Life's Tapestry

Other titles by Martin Goldsmith:
Islam and Christian Witness
What About Other Faiths? (Hodder & Stoughton)
Your Guide to Guidance (IVP)

Other titles by Elizabeth Goldsmith:
Getting There From Here
God Can Be Trusted

Life's Tapestry

Reflections and Insights from my Life

MARTIN GOLDSMITH

Authentic
LIFESTYLE

Copyright © 1997 Martin Goldsmith

First published 1997 by OM Publishing

Reprinted 2000, 2003, 2006, 2008

14 13 12 11 10 09 08   11 10 9 8 7 6 5

Authentic Media, 9 Holdom Avenue, Bletchley,
Milton Keynes, Bucks MK1 1QR
1820 Jet Stream Drive, Colorado Springs, CO 80921, USA
OM Authentic Media, Medchal Road, Jeedimetla Village,
Secunderabad 500 055, A.P., India
www.authenticmedia.co.uk
Authentic Media is a division of IBS-STL U.K., limited by guarantee,
with its Registered Office at Kingstown Broadway, Carlisle,
Cumbria CA3 0HA. Registered in England & Wales No. 1216232.
Registered charity 270162

British Library Cataloguing in Publication Data

A catalogue record for this book is available from the
British Library

ISBN 978-1-85078-273-5

Typeset by WestKey Ltd, Falmouth
and printed in the UK by Mackays of Chatham PLC, Kent

Table of Contents

Foreword

I remember as a girl we would travel to one place and the people there would introduce my dad as an expert in a given field. They would quiz him and he would sparkle.

On the next occasion a new body of people would want to draw out from him a completely different wisdom. Most seemed unaware that he was equally brilliant on a whole range of subjects untapped by them.

The joy of this book is that his remarkable breadth of experience can be taken in. You'll laugh and cry, you'll be inspired and you'll be rebuked.

I used to tell my dad that I knew his favourite sermons off by heart, including the jokes! So it's refreshing in this book not to be preached at, but to be *voyeurs* of the experiences and emotions that have shaped a man with such a heart after God.

As you read his stories you will realize that he is an evangelist and a theologian, a pioneer and a truly humble man. But to me, he's my dad, and in his loving fathering he's passed on to me all that is most valuable in life. I believe that as you read this book he'll pass on much of value to you as well.

Margaret Ellis

Introduction

'Stay under the table. You're a missionary!'

Using a vivid Indonesian expression my friend was firmly reminding me that my role in the church in North Sumatra, Indonesia, was 'under the table', the behind-the-scenes ministry of teaching, encouraging, motivating and stimulating. Happily a natural chemistry had drawn the leading church elder and me together in a trusting relationship which allowed him the freedom to speak so candidly to me. In post-colonial Indonesia it was particularly important for the national Christians to assert their independence of foreign missionary leadership and regain the true confidence that they could not only maintain their churches themselves, but also move out in dynamic evangelism and church planting without foreigners to direct them.

What then was the occasion of this reminder? My

wife and I had bicycled out from our town through the beautiful local scenery dominated by the impressive volcano with smoke constantly issuing from its crater. We visited a nearby village with some four thousand inhabitants in order to enjoy the beauty of its huge eight-family traditional houses. Topped with sago-palm thatching on their decoratively shaped roofs and with fearsome waterbuffalo horns at either end of the roof to warn off potential enemies, these houses drew out from us the longing that their interior darkness might be filled with a new light through the good news of Jesus Christ.

On our arrival in the village we were soon invited to share glasses of tea and coffee with a crowd of local people who were curious to know who we were and why we had come to their village. We later discovered that this village had a formidable reputation as the very traditional centre for the old religion of the Karo Batak people. 'Yes, you should go to Lingga', the old head of the Karo Batak church later advised us, 'you will really get to understand our culture there.'

But the crowd around us soon began to ask questions about Jesus Christ. After much discussion the local school master begged us to return regularly and teach them the Christian faith. 'We promise you that several hundred of us will believe and become Christians if you will come and teach us', he said.

We were excited at the prospect of planting a church of such numbers in such a place and quickly went to our church elder friend to tell him the good news. He informed us that his forefathers all came from that village and he still had many relatives there, as did several other leading Christians in our town. Our going to the village of Lingga and our vision for church planting stimulated these local Christians to go themselves to start a church there. Under their leadership this grew rapidly and developed its own strong leadership. And the church in Lingga then planted churches in other nearby villages. Both Muslims and followers of the traditional religion came to faith in Christ.

We learned a vital lesson too, which has influenced our whole life. We had looked forward to returning to Lingga to lead a church planting team and pioneer a new church there. But our friend had reminded us that it was important for us to remain behind the scenes and thus allow local believers to take the lead, do the work and thus gain confidence in ministry. If we had taken the lead, there would also have been the inevitable danger that the message of Christ would have been shrouded in a western cloak and the Christian gospel would have seemed foreign. With some regret we had to stay in the background.

So we learned that God has called us to challenge and encourage others in local churches to do the work of evangelism, church planting, teaching and training Christians. We therefore particularly rejoice when we hear of missionaries overseas who are working in and under the leadership of local churches in order to motivate them to serve the Lord. We note the importance of this principle in the British church also where the task of ministers or church leaders must fundamentally be to teach, train and mobilize all the church members — otherwise the ministers will have nervous breakdowns trying to do everything themselves! We were so encouraged when we first returned to Britain after our years overseas. We had the great privilege of being part of a large Anglican Church where the minister humbly encouraged the church members to do the work of evangelism, pastor each other and share the scriptures with each other. He knew how to delegate and encourage while he led from behind. No wonder the church flourished and grew!

It was with this background in our minds that my wife and I recently discussed together the meaning of a 'prophecy' which Gerald Coates of Pioneer People had given us. In it he stressed the word 'legacy', that we should leave something significant behind for future generations. In his grace God has given us lives with much wide and rich experience, preaching and lecturing in many countries in every continent. Should we therefore try to pass on to others some of the lessons God has been trying to teach us?

My first reactions were mixed. We wanted to be open to God and agreed we must wait to see what would develop. We know that all our 'words from God' contain some human input as well as being inspired by the Holy Spirit. They therefore need to be discerned. Then also in the light of our fundamental calling to remain 'under the table' we felt that God has already allowed us to leave something of a legacy which will continue to bear fruit even after we have died. During almost a quarter century of teaching at All Nations Christian College we have been allowed to have some input into the lives of many young professionals who are now serving the Lord and his church all over the world. And we are often encour-

aged when we see what former All Nations graduates
are doing, even in tough situations in countries like
Afghanistan. Likewise, in our wider preaching and
lecturing ministry both in Britain and overseas, God
has wonderfully spoken to some people and set their
feet on new paths of commitment to and service of the
Lord. Any legacy we may have must flow primarily
through the lives of other people, not lie in our own
achievements.

And yet the Holy Spirit has not allowed us to forget
the idea of 'legacy'. Was God speaking to us through
Gerald Coates's challenge? Over the months since that
time we have begun seriously to consider the possibility
of writing down something of the lessons that have
come through forty years of Christian experience and
service. It is now our prayer that this book may indeed
pass on a legacy which will be of help to the generations
which follow us.

Despite the amazingly rich experience which God
has led us through in our lives, it is still with considerable hesitation that I put pen to paper to share it with
others. What right do I have to ask other people to
learn from my 'legacy'? In answer to this question I can
only share another experience in Indonesia which has
warmly encouraged us.

When we were still new in Indonesia back in the early
1960s a very large church in our area faced horrendous
internal struggles. Two millionaires were striving to gain
the upper hand in the church. One Sunday the huge
congregation in our neighbouring city split down the
middle. Half the congregation supported one minister
and the other half gave allegiance to a second man. One

minister backed the one millionaire while the other man belonged to the other millionaire's faction. That Sunday the congregation became violent as they fought to push their particular minister into the pulpit. People were getting hurt and the police were called. They carted one of the ministers away, thrusting the other into the pulpit to take the Sunday service. At the foot of the high pulpit stood armed policemen to ensure peace during the service. The minister preached an evangelistic sermon and amazingly some people found new life in Christ through his preaching that morning.

I was bewildered. Does God not use clean vessels in his service? How could God's Holy Spirit work so powerfully when sin so obviously reigned? It was with such questions in my mind that I went to ask advice from an Indonesian friend.

Instead of answering my questions he countered them with this searching question of his own. 'Does God ever bring people to faith in Christ through British ministers?'

'How like Jesus!', I thought afterwards. 'He often answered questions by asking one himself.'

I admitted that occasionally it does happen that British ministers channel the work of God's Spirit to others. I didn't need to say anything more. I knew what he meant. Are British preachers so sinless and perfect? Are the sins of British church leaders of less weight in God's eyes than the sins of those Indonesian Christians?

Of course God wants us all to be holy even as he is holy. Of course it is the work of the Holy Spirit to change us into the image of God and make us holy. But amazingly God puts his glory into mere earthen vessels and uses sinful men and women to glorify his name. In my life I have found this such an encouragement. In his grace God will even use little people like us with all our inadequacies, failures and sin.

That is why I have the temerity to pass on my 'legacy' to others in this book. In our lives God's teaching has been wonderful; our learning has been slow and faltering; but our confidence is that God patiently continues to lead us and we look forward to that great day when we shall know him perfectly and we shall be fully like him. What a future we all have as Christians! May my 'legacy' play some part in encouraging us all as we walk towards that future! The past is a superb introduction to the future.

Chapter 1

Learning to Know God

Through the Bible

I have always enjoyed reading. Books have played an important part in my development as a child and indeed throughout my life. So it came about one day when I was about eleven that I was investigating the fascinating rows of books in a sitting-room bookcase. To my surprise I came across one which evidently belonged to me. I read the inscription on the first page: 'To Martin with all my love and best wishes, Auntie Kathleen.'

It was an old book covered in black leather bearing the title 'Holy Bible'. The date next to the inscription showed that it had been given to me eleven years before, when I was just a baby. Doubtless it had remained unread all those years, gathering dust on the bookshelf.

As a family we had spent the five years of the second

World War abroad and all our furniture had been stored to await our return to England. Now we had a new home in Hove on the south coast of England and so the books also emerged from the dustsheets to find their proper places on the shelves.

What an unexpected excitement to find something that actually belonged to me! I immediately took it up to my bedroom and thus began my lifelong story of getting to know God.

While some people naughtily glance at the last chapters of detective novels, I had been well trained always to start books at the beginning and carefully read them right through to the end. So I began to read the Bible at the first chapter of Genesis; then on to Exodus — Leviticus — Numbers and on until I reached the end. I was fascinated. I knew that our family came from a Jewish background, but had no idea what that really meant. But here in this book was the story of the Jewish people, starting right from the beginning with the creation of the world. And the whole book was written by Jews and had such an amazingly Jewish character. It gripped me. Looking back, I can now understand how this was the miraculous working of the Holy Spirit. He it was who caused me to be so fascinated by this old King James version of the Bible with its out-dated English language. Of course there was so much that a young eleven-year-old boy could not hope to understand, but that did not put me off. Even the intricate details of the sacrificial system in the book of Leviticus gripped my attention.

After returning from overseas I was sent to a boarding school for boys. Here we were all made to sit quietly each evening for three quarters of an hour in a classroom. During this time we could read whatever we wanted, but we had to read a book (not a comic!). Other boys indulged in 'classics' like Biggles or other boys' adventure books, but I read solemnly through the Bible again and again. It was not that I was a pious youngster at all, for we were not a very religious family. In fact I did not think of the Bible as a religious book and did not consciously associate it in any way with church. I read it because I enjoyed it and was so enthralled by its contents that I could not leave it aside.

Gradually the message of the Bible percolated through my mind. I began to see something of who God was, what he was like, what sort of things he did for Israel and for Christians, what pleases him and what makes him angry and unhappy. So I was beginning to know something about God, but it did not occur to me that I could have any sort of personal relationship with him or that he would do anything in my life. To me the Bible was like a historical biography. As you read about Napoleon or some other historical character, you get to know quite a lot about him and you also identify with him, putting yourself into his shoes. But you do not think that you might actually meet this hero of history.

This failure to realize that God might actually want to call me into a living relationship with himself was related also to my own personal background. My father died just before I was born. My mother brought me up to believe that my father was a special person. As a child I always kept a photo of him by my bedside and would always kiss him good night. I loved my

father deeply and admired him tremendously as someone of outstanding excellence, but of course I never
actually knew him and he never spoke back to me when
I said 'good night' to him.

Was God like that too? It was only many years later
that I realized that my relationship to God the Father
was influenced by this background with my human
father. When I became a committed Christian, I loved
God the Father and thought he was absolutely wonderful in all his splendour and glory. But I found it
difficult to relate intimately to him even though I loved,
worshipped and served him with all my heart. I could
relate to the more human Jesus Christ and to the very
intimate Holy Spirit, but the Father remained 'the
invisible God' (Col.1:15). This has helped me in more
recent years to get alongside people whose relationship
with God is also knowingly or unknowingly influenced
by their experience of their human fathers.

Nevertheless God was laying good foundations in
my life. About once a year I read the whole Bible
through from Genesis to Revelation and then would
begin again at the beginning. It was not yet applied to
my life and I did not grasp some of the great truths of
the Bible, but the overall nature of a true biblical faith
was taking root in my understanding.

Through a miracle

When thirteen years old I moved to another school and
thus began a deeply unhappy period of my life. And
yet when I look back at what happened, I can only

thank God that the tears were the introduction to new life.

On moving to this new boarding school I quickly became terribly unpopular. The next couple of years were overshadowed by continual bullying and teasing. There was no refuge to which I could escape for peace, for everything was done communally in the school. Even in the evenings I could not run back to home and parents for protection and security, for this was a boarding school. As a result I became miserably un-happy with a deep sense of insecurity. I felt unloved and indeed unworthy of being loved.

My one escape route lay in books. Whenever possi-ble I hid away in the school library where I devoured a host of books. And quietly I went on reading the Bible through and through.

One evening I was reading the Bible in bed and new thoughts crept gradually into my mind. At first they seemed so ridiculous that they were dismissed. But still these new thoughts kept pressing in. Could it really be possible? Probably not, but it was worth trying. In this way my first conscious prayer found faltering expres-sion.

'God, if you still work miracles for people, please would you give me twenty-four hours when no one will say or do anything to me.'

Was God, the hero of the Bible, still alive? Does he still intervene amazingly and spectacularly in the lives of ordinary human beings? If so, would he really be interested in doing something for an insignificant fifteen-year-old lad like me? It all seemed rather unlikely.

The following day dawned just like any other day. Breakfast, chapel, school classes, lunch, football, homework, evening meal, more homework and time in the common room with all the other boys of my house.

But this day was different. The routine programme of school life remained the same as always, but it seemed as if I did not exist. No one seemed to notice me in any way. No boy talked to me at all. No one asked me to pass the salt or clear the table during meals. Likewise no master said or did anything in relationship to me. Nobody took a register in class, asked me a question or addressed any word to me. In the afternoon I played football, but no one called to me to pass the ball — perhaps they knew I was not very good at football and so it was not worth asking!

As the twenty-four hours passed I became excitedly aware of what was happening. I was agog to see whether it would continue. God was answering my prayer. In fact he was doing more than I had intended. In my prayer I had meant to ask that no one would do anything bad to me, that no one would tease me or bully me. But God took my words quite literally. I had asked him that no one should say or do anything to me — and indeed no one said a single word to me and no one did anything which directly related to me.

God had proved himself to me. He is still alive. He does still work miracles for his people. And he is interested even in little people like me. What a God!

At the end of the twenty-four hours I made my way quietly to the school chapel. I somehow felt that solemn transactions with God should be sealed in the chapel. It was absolutely dark and I was quite alone. It was a long slender building with seats facing each other in long rows the whole length of the chapel. At the end facing the sanctuary a flight of stairs led down into the long aisle. I stood in the dark at the top of the stairs and prayed aloud in the lofty silence:

'God, you have shown me that you are alive and you are great. I want my life to belong to you. Please accept me and I promise to follow you with all that I have.' I cannot remember exactly what words I used in my prayer that evening, but I determined to live for God from then on.

From the outset of this new phase in my life I knew that God could do miracles and that he was excitingly alive. But I had no idea what it really meant to become a Christian. In spite of having read the whole Bible through some five times by then, I still did not understand the real significance of the death and resurrection of Jesus Christ.

So I set out to be religious. The chapel became central to my life at school and at home too I began to go to church. I wanted to serve and to please God; going frequently to chapel seemed the right way to do so. I wanted also to become a good person because I knew that God hates all forms of evil. But I had no understanding of the Christian concept of grace and I did not know how the Holy Spirit could give me a power for holiness in my life. Everything seemed to depend on my own resolve and my own effort to please God and to serve him.

As might be expected, this stage of my Christian life was not altogether a great success. I failed God again and again. Outwardly there seemed to be little sign of spiritual change or new life in Christ. Nevertheless I am confident that this was when I became a Christian and began the new life which has led on to so much more in the years that followed.

This background has made me very aware that people may in fact be true Christians even when they seem quite nominal in their faith, untaught in their biblical understanding and even rather unsanctified in their Christian lives. God is so patient and leads us forward step by step.

Through spiritual experiences

My time at school came to an end in a blaze of exams and cricket, knowing that serious adult life loomed on the horizon. In those days all young men in Britain had to do two years military service. Suddenly cricket cap and blazer gave way to naval uniform and new challenges burst into our immature lives.

The first challenge came immediately on arrival in the big dormitory where all the new recruits of our intake slept. I met the man who had the next bed and we began to laugh together in an immediate friendship. The Petty Officer in charge entered the dormitory, noted our laughing, stalked the length of the room and stood threateningly before us.

'If you're still laughing in a week's time I'll give you a shilling', he growled menacingly.

Would we be able to keep our heads above water in the pressures of initial naval training? Could God keep me laughing in the midst of purposefully tough discipline?

One week later we were all in the dormitory one evening and suddenly the Petty Officer appeared again. He stalked down to my friend and myself. With a scowl he tossed a shilling onto my bed and said, 'I owe you that'. Then he marched out of the room.

We were on a special course which trained us to become interpreters in the Russian language. After the initial training the slog of language study began in earnest. Long lists of vocabulary awaited us each day. We ate, drank and slept Russian, Russian, Russian all day every day. Every two weeks we faced exams — and two failures meant dismissal from the course. Very few of us survived to the end of the interpreters' course, although some were allowed to stay on for the lower level translators' course. In about twenty months they pushed us through from learning the first letter of the Russian alphabet to the final exam to qualify as full interpreters.

During these years in the navy I struggled to continue following God and joined what was then called the United Naval Christian Fellowship. This was my first experience of being together with evangelical Christians and it felt good.

The UNCF had a hospitality list with names and addresses of families who were happy to welcome sailors into their home. Before we began our Russian studies I served for a while on a destroyer and we docked for a few days in Devonport. There I looked at the hospitality list, found a home that was open to us and visited it. The family were so warm in their welcome and I immediately sensed the loving atmosphere of a Christian home. A new seed was planted into my life. If ever I got married, I wanted a home like that.

But once our Russian studies began, life revolved around things Russian — Russian language, Russian culture, Russian politics, Russian people, Russian religion. And so began my experience of the Russian Orthodox Church.

The meaningful beauty of the liturgy and the deep harmonies of the worship music enthralled me. I can understand without difficulty what the envoys of the Russian tsar Vladimir felt a thousand years ago when they visited the great Orthodox Church of St. Sophia in Constantinople. They exclaimed in awe 'We did not know whether we were in heaven or on earth. We only knew that their God dwells among men.'

When I attended the Russian Orthodox Church the reality and presence of God became inescapably real. The symbolism of the liturgy and the emotive music have kept the Russian church alive right through the seventy years of fierce communist persecution in the Soviet Union, and they played a significant part in bringing spiritual life to me too.

Often in the Russian church in Oxford we had visits from men who had been monks for many years. They were rugged men whose gnarled fingers and tough weather-beaten faces testified to their long years of solitude and utter simplicity. I did not ask about their theological understanding or the tenets of their biblical faith, but as an evangelical I can imagine that there might well have been some weaknesses. But these were men who knew God intimately, who had lived alone with him as their sole companion, who lived for God alone. Such spirituality impressed me deeply and has influenced my whole life ever since.

I often wonder whether it is really feasible to combine the Orthodox beauty of music and their enacted symbolism of liturgy with an evangelical biblical faith and the dynamic of life in the Holy Spirit.

One professor at Oxford came near to typifying this before my eyes. Nadejda Gorodetskaya lectured us on the writings of Tolstoi. In her lectures she portrayed the religious life and faith of Tolstoi and in this way she boldly and unhesitatingly shared her own living faith. As a young student I was influenced by her and sometimes shared with her.

However at Oxford the magnet of vital evangelical faith pulled me compellingly into its orbit. While thanking God for the impressive spiritual influence of the Russian Orthodox in my life, I became increasingly uneasy with their reverence of Mary, the saints and the icons. God had used the Orthodox Church in my development and its influence would remain permanently with me, but now the compass of God's purposes pointed excitingly in new directions.

Through grace

During my first weekend at Oxford Maurice Wood (later to become Bishop of Norwich) preached a powerful evangelistic sermon for the Christian Union. God the Holy Spirit convicted me overwhelmingly that this was God's word for me. It felt as if nothing else in the world had any significance at that moment — God was speaking personally to me.

'Behold, I stand at the door and knock; if any one hears my voice and opens the door, I will come in to him and eat with him, and he with me' (Rev. 3:20).

When God speaks so definitely, you cannot but respond. I was overwhelmed by the presence of God and the knowledge that he wanted to come into my life. I knew that life could never be the same again. This was a radical turning-point because from now on the reality of God's glory could not be doubted.

The intense experience of God's presence and his speaking to me meant that I was hardly aware of the metaphor of God knocking or his call to open the door. Actually the idea of God knocking should have been very obvious because Maurice Wood timed his sermon to perfection. He knew that the great bell called Big Tom resounds through the church at 8.55 p.m. and in his sermon God began to knock at the door precisely as the bell began to toll. And Big Tom strikes a hundred and one times, so God knocked a hundred and one times in the sermon! But I did not notice this.

So it came as a big surprise when the older student who had taken me to this evangelistic meeting asked me:

'Martin, have you opened the door?' By then we were in his room; it was a damp autumn evening before the modern luxuries of central heating.

'How can one enter an Oxford room without opening the door', I thought to myself with some bewilderment. If you don't open the door, you hit your nose! I began to feel ill at ease with my friend. But worse was to follow.

'Would you like something to drink?' he asked me. I had only recently left service in the navy and was hard-drinking and my language was also rather lurid. The 'drink' offered to me turned out to be Horlicks! The only person in the world I knew who drank Horlicks was an old great aunt.

This communication failure led to it being reported in a Christian Union prayer meeting that 'Goldsmith was hopeless'.

Despite my new experience of God's presence I still had not grasped the significance of Jesus' cross and resurrection as the only means of life and salvation in relationship with God. But my heart was hungrily open and now another fellow-student burst into my life. He was challenged by the report that I was hopeless, believing that with God no one is beyond God's reach. He therefore determined prayerfully to make contact with me.

Colin Jee radiated unbounded enthusiasm for the Christian faith. In his witness to other students he broke every possible rule on how to witness, but his joyful excitement and commitment as a Christian impressed and challenged all with whom he came into contact.

One evening I went into the college dining hall for the evening meal and happened to sit next to Colin. We had never met before, but he quickly engaged me in conversation in a warm, friendly way.

Almost immediately he asked me without any sign of embarrassment,

'Do you know Jesus Christ?'

After a moment's surprise and shock at such a direct and unconventional question I stumblingly tried to reply. I noted right away that he seemed to have an intimate relationship with God which attracted me. This was what I had been searching for ever since that miraculous answer to prayer six years before when I was fifteen. He invited me to his room to talk further.

When he served us coffee in his room he confessed with no sign of awkwardness that he had only one biscuit! He insisted that I have it. His cheerful manner and his obvious enthusiasm made it easy to talk openly and to look at the Bible together. He showed me verse after verse in the Bible to demonstrate the meaning of Jesus' cross and resurrection for sinners like us. I was impressed at his ability to find verses from all over the Bible. I had been reading the Bible through and through from Genesis to Revelation for ten years, but I didn't know individual verses like that. In this way he showed me that the key to the Christian faith is not what we do for God, but rather what God has done for us. He explained to me how the totally perfect, sinless Jesus had taken the penalty for our sins and had died for us and in our place. He went on to show how by faith we can be united to Jesus in his resurrection and so have a new resurrection life which is like being born again. Through these very basic and simple biblical truths all my religious struggles began to take on new meaning and things made sense.

Like most British people I don't accept new things immediately. However impressed I might be, I wanted to check it out. Was what Colin said really in line with the overall message of the Bible? I knew this was what I needed and wanted, but could I really be sure?

So I began to reread the Bible from the beginning to see whether Colin's explanations fitted. I had already read it through some ten times over the years, but now the multi-coloured bits of the jigsaw began to fit together and a glorious picture took shape. The word 'grace' seemed to shine like a guiding beacon as I read. The reality that the creator God in all his burning holiness and glorious splendour should love a little person like me with all my inadequacy and sin — what grace!

During that year when I was checking out this wonderful new idea of grace through Christ's cross and resurrection I began also to join with other evangelical Christians in the Christian Union. Fellowship with other Christians and regular biblical teaching showed me that this was where I belonged. I began also to attend a good evangelical Anglican Church where love and biblical teaching combined to help us all to grow as Christians.

The minister of that church channelled part of his spiritual wisdom into my life and still today I often look back and thank God for the legacy he handed down to me from his many years of ministry in Oxford. Basil Gough was a saintly and down-to-earth practical Christian leader. I learned much from him which has been formative in my life.

One summer vacation I had a job lined up, but just before the end of the summer term it fell through and I was left with the prospect of three months' vacation with nothing particular to do. I consulted with Basil

Gough, asking his advice. He suggested that I spend a fortnight as part of an evangelistic team who were involved in a church mission in order to get some practical Christian experience. The other suggestion was that I should spend the whole vacation carefully studying Paul's letter to the Romans. What a foundation for a Christian life! I can recommend it! That vacation I duly spent some six hours a day with open commentaries beside the actual text of Romans. Much time was also given to praying through each verse and passage I studied, so that the text was applied to my own life and to those for whom I prayed. John Stott in his Bible Speaks Today commentary on Romans details five leading Christians in church history for whom the book of Romans was formative. I don't know whether Basil Gough was thinking of them when he advised me to study Romans in detail at this early stage of my Christian life. In any case it was good advice. And since then I have followed his example and made the same suggestion to some younger students when they have been wondering what to do in their long university summer vacation.

Basil Gough also gave me very practical and detailed advice on the use of Sundays while I was at university. Again I have passed on this advice to others since then, carefully emphasizing that we should not be slavishly legalistic about it. He suggested a quiet prayerful breakfast in my room at 8.30 or 9 a.m. with time afterwards for a good period of prayer and Bible reading before going to church for the morning service. He then thought it might be good to save time by fasting and so have ample space for more time with the

Lord through until mid-afternoon. Then he advised time together with another Christian in fellowship or with a non-Christian with witness in mind. In those days it was customary for Christians to attend church in the evening as well as the morning on Sundays; and the Christian Union always held an evangelistic meeting and sermon at 8 p.m. each Sunday, so we all tried to invite people to come with us to that and otherwise we just went ourselves in order to pray.

Basil Gough's third piece of advice which I have never forgotten was also very practical. He would have doubted the idea that Christians have a 'spirit of laziness' which needs to be cast out by prayer. He felt that the clue to a successful Christian life lay in a Bible and an alarm clock. He strongly recommended the discipline of getting up in good time in order to be with the Lord in regular prayer and Bible study.

Basil Gough influenced me not only by his fatherly spirituality and his words of practical advice. He also said something to me from his long years of experience in ministry with Oxford university students. He had noticed that students who are uncompromising and appear fanatical at university with all the immaturity and lack of wisdom of new Christians, broaden out as the years pass and become godly mature Christians of clear biblical faith. But he observed that students who were wise, mature and balanced when young became theologically rather liberal with a lack of vital biblical witness. Now that I am older I often remember his wise observation and it helps me to be more tolerant of the unwise enthusiasm and fanaticism of younger

Christians — and indeed I rejoice in their dynamic and vitality.

Through prayer

My Christian life began with the combination of reading the Bible and experiencing the reality of God answering my prayer in miraculous ways. Now in Oxford biblical teaching on prayer gripped my heart.

'Whatever you ask in my name, I will do it', Jesus promised. And in order to emphasize what he said, he then repeated it in very slightly differing words (John 14: 13–14). 'And this is the confidence which we have in him, that if we ask anything according to his will he hears us. And if we know that he hears us in whatever we ask, we know that we have obtained the requests made of him' (1 John 5:14–15).

These and other similar promises in the New Testament gave me a supreme confidence in prayer. I had no doubt that God would automatically grant me whatever I asked him in prayer. And my confidence was well placed. God kept his promises fully in those early days of my new evangelical faith. As I look back on those days, I blush. I was so immature and lacking in understanding. But God is so gracious and he knows what his children need at each stage of our lives.

During my third year at Oxford I had a room at the very top of the house. The staircase had no windows and it was therefore impossible to see out when going up or downstairs. Each week I had a tutorial in the home of one of my professors who lived a good way out from the centre of the city where I had my room. So my faith was tested when it rained and I would pray before leaving my room to go downstairs,

'Lord, please stop the rain before I get downstairs and have to bicycle out for my tutorial'.

In faith I would leave my raincoat behind in my room in the assurance that God would answer prayer — and he did again and again! So I asked the Lord for all sorts of miracles in those days and God in his goodness gave me these signs of his reality and of his love for me. He knew that I was immature and needed such proofs of his faithfulness.

But then one day I was reading my Bible and one verse seemed to jump out of the page and impressed itself upon me. 'We walk by faith, not by sight' (2 Cor. 5:7). I knew immediately what God wanted to say to me. It was time for me to grow up in my Christian life, so that I should not be so spiritually dependent on visible signs of the reality and love of God. I needed to learn to walk by faith and trust the Lord even when apparently he did not do what I wanted.

Later in my life I read books by the Japanese author Kosuke Koyama in which he emphasizes the danger of 'domesticating' God, turning God into our servant who will obediently do whatever we want. We can so easily try to use God as if he were like the genie in Aladdin's lamp. The genie responds obediently when we rub the lamp with our prayers and he says to us, 'At your service, master.' God cannot be so tamed or 'domesticated'—he is almighty God and we exist to serve and glorify him rather than the other way round. I needed to learn that lesson.

In his grace God allowed me to go through a stage of life in which it seemed that God never answered prayer. In fact, it sometimes seemed rather dangerous to pray for something because then it was sure not to come about — the more I prayed, the less things happened! God was beginning to teach me the hard lesson of loving and trusting him whatever the circumstances — a useful lesson later in my life when I worked as a missionary overseas.

Through God's working

Despite the lesson of walking 'by faith, not by sight' the reality of God working miraculously and answering prayer still formed a vital part of my Christian life and of my expectations. And God used those years at Oxford to build good foundations for my future life as a missionary. God knows from the start what we all need for the life and work to which he is leading us.

The glorious reality of God's grace as the basis of my relationship with God changed my life. I was tremendously excited by the assurance that God loved me, that God wanted me as his child, that through the cross and resurrection of Christ he had cleansed me and given me a new life with him. Partly because of the bullying I had experienced as a youngster I had become rather insecure and unsure of myself. I also grew up in the shadow of my older brother who was obviously cleverer than me, so from time to time my teachers had compared me unfavourably with him. But now I knew that almighty God had chosen me to be his beloved child. It thrilled me that *God himself* could want me and this gave me a new self-confidence. Even my football improved! Instead of drawing back from tackling anyone lest I cause offence, I now threw myself into a game with new confidence. Of course it was not only in unimportant details like football where God began to change me!

Although I was now beginning to learn to walk by faith, God still went on working. He not only worked in me but also showed me that he could work through me.

In those days Worcester College, Oxford was known for its social and rather strongly public school background. We had a reputation for being not very academic, but good at sport and consuming considerable quantities of alcohol. Respectable religion in the college chapel could be tolerated, but life-changing personal faith in a living Lord was generally felt to be too 'fanatical'. On the other hand many students had a background of religious teaching and chapel worship which just needed to be set on fire through a personal experience of God.

In the Christian Union great emphasis was laid on evangelism. Since I had come into a new and exciting knowledge of Christ it was assumed that God would want to use me to lead others into faith in Jesus Christ. My new friend Colin Jee showed me verses from the Bible which I could use to help others understand the basic truths of the Christian faith and how they could become true Christians. With great enthusiasm I passed on what I learned and what I experienced. And wonderfully the Holy Spirit used that witness to lead other students one after another to faith in Christ.

One weekend Billy Graham came to take evangelistic meetings in Oxford. We were all praying for many to be converted through that weekend. Then we felt in our little Worcester College group that surely God wanted to use us too, not just Billy Graham. So we began to pray that more students in our college would come to faith before the weekend than during or after it. God honoured that prayer. Twelve new people were added to our group before the weekend and a further eight after it. It was exciting to see God working in changing other people's lives. What a privilege it was to play one's own part in God's work! By the end of that year twenty-five per cent of Worcester College students had come to faith in the Lord and had linked up with the Christian Union.

As the academic year came towards its close, students began to pray about the long summer vacation. 'Lord, please help us to remain spiritually warm even when we are away from the spiritual life and teaching here in Oxford. Lord, we shall miss the fellowship here, and Lord, it's a long time to have to exist without all that you give us here in Oxford.'

This sort of prayer seemed wrong to me. Could not God use us equally in our home towns and churches? Does he not have a missionary purpose when he allows us the long months of summer vacation at home? Does our faith depend on the Christian Union in Oxford? If it does, what will happen when we leave Oxford and are immersed in the 'real world', not just for three or four months but for the rest of our lives?

So I began to pray not only that God would continue to build up my Christian life while at home, but also that he would use me in my home church. My church in Hove, Sussex was at that time not very alive spiritually. The vicar was warm hearted with a deep and enthusiastic knowledge of God, but he was rather afraid of anything evangelical and had no training in how to preach effectively from the Bible. The church languished in the visionless and lifeless round of maintaining the status quo.

God led me to pray that I might lead one local young man and one local young woman to faith in Jesus Christ. God answered the prayer he had inspired. What a thrill it was to lead these two excellent young people to Christ! Whenever I was at home for vacations we met together to pray and study the Bible together. We so enjoyed each other and the rich fellowship God gave us as young Christians. What I learned at Oxford I passed on to them, for I was only one step ahead of them in faith. Then they began to lead others to Christ and we developed a Bible study group. As the years went by, they led many of the church's activities and were elected onto the church council. So in due course Holy Trinity, Hove became a definitely evangelical church. Several of these young people went on to be ordained into the Anglican ministry.

God was teaching me a lesson. He can bring new life into a church through the one-to-one witness of even a new young Christian with no official standing or position in the church.

But I did miss the warm fellowship at Oxford. Often when I walked along the sea front in Hove I would observe all the other people on the promenade to see if there might be another Christian among them. In those days Christians often wore special Christian badges in their lapel, so I carefully looked out for a Scripture Union, Crusader or other Christian badge. It is a mark of living faith in Christ that we come to love our fellow-Christians, for 'we know that we have passed out of death into life, because we love the brethren' (1 John 3:14).

Looking back on my life, it seems like a paradox. Even while God was teaching me to walk by faith and not just by sight, still he graciously continued to work miraculously in and through me. But the sensational miracle-seeking prayers of my very early days at Oxford now ceased because God no longer responded to such prayers.

Later in life I was to learn another lesson about walking by sight and by faith. I was invited to speak at a large pan-European youth missions conference and was deeply disturbed by the dynamic talks given by the other main speaker.

'Every Christian ought to experience supernatural miracles every day', he reiterated. And he carefully defined the word 'supernatural' to show that he meant exactly what he said. He emphasized that not only he himself, but everyone of us should experience such supernatural miracles every day without exception. I worried about the effect this might have on the crowds of often insecure young people there. Would they become discouraged and disillusioned? I shared my concerns with a wise and godly missionary who was leading seminars at the conference. I told him my experience of learning to walk by faith, not just by sight. He had the opposite experience. He had grown up in a lovely godly Christian home centred on prayer, Bible reading and holy upright living. But now in middle age God had been showing him something new — God could also answer prayer miraculously and miracles could still be the order of the day. So he was learning to walk by sight and not just by faith! Together we came to realize that God wants all his children to have a full-orbed knowledge and experience of himself.

Through a system

In those early days at university we were taught somewhat rigid systems of how to evangelize and how to disciple a younger believer. We were given particular verses to teach particular truths in a definite order. We knew Bible verses by heart which demonstrated the great foundational truths of the gospel — human sin, repentance, the atoning work of the cross, the life giving resurrection, justification by faith, receiving the Holy Spirit etc. Likewise when we did lead someone into faith in Christ, we were encouraged to meet weekly with them in order to help them grow in their new faith. Each meeting together would begin and end with prayer. We knew what biblical passages would be helpful to read together with a new Christian.

I was reminded of these rather rigid systems later when I tried to teach my son how to drive. I soon realized that he needed detailed instructions with a definite set order of what to do when. I had long since forgotten whether you turn the engine on first before you look in the mirror, signal, check the brakes etc. Only when a beginner has mastered these detailed patterns of driving can one learn to be more flexible according to the situation one faces, starting the car in one's own garage or in a crowded street. Of course with experience the rigid system gives way to easy flexibility — but a set system is essential to get the beginner started.

So many Christians do not dare to witness for Christ or lead their friends to faith in the Lord. Is it because they do not have a basic system to give them confidence? Of course one hopes that all Christians will grow beyond set systems into more sensitive person-related approaches, but all of us need basic patterns to begin with.

In many ways God used my university years to lay the foundations for the life and ministry to which God was going to call me.

Chapter 2

The Next Step — Training and Marriage

God calls

'You are a keen linguist and keen Christian, you'll presumably become a missionary', someone said to me quite early on in my time at Oxford. Soon afterwards someone else sent me a letter rejoicing in the new life-changing experience of Christ and his grace which had set me on fire for the Lord in those days. The letter went on to note that I was not only now a keen Christian, but also happened to be an enthusiastic linguist. My friend drew the obvious conclusion that I would become a missionary.

And so it went on. Person after person assumed that overseas missionary work naturally followed if one loved the Lord and enjoyed languages. At first I smiled gently and pointed out that many keen Christians who also studied languages did not become missionaries. The next time I replied more strongly that there is no inevitable consequence from the mathematical formula of missionary plus linguist. After several such encounters I began to get quite angry when such suggestions were made to me.

'Argument weak, shout louder'. I began to notice that this old proverb fitted my situation.

But I didn't want to become a missionary overseas. I had settled happily into British life after our five years in Bermuda when I was a child. I had no desire to live overseas again. England had become my home.

Nor did I know anything about missionary work. The whole idea was quite beyond my horizons. It was at that stage that the college chaplain invited a missionary from Africa to speak in our college. Although it was nothing to do with the Christian Union it seemed right to attend.

The missionary turned out to be rather old and out of touch with modern English student life. He came from an extreme Anglo-Catholic background and was working in a rural situation somewhere in Africa. My only memory of this meeting is one or two of the slides he showed of himself in full clerical vestments followed by a line of African porters carrying his boxes. I remember that he asked us to pray for missionaries because it is so hot in a tropical climate when one has to wear all those vestments!

I could not quite imagine myself fitting into this picture of missionary life and work. So I strongly resisted the pressure to accept a call to missionary service. But the more I rejected God's increasingly clear call, the more I lost my sense of peace. It became increasingly difficult to pray, the Bible lost its illuminating power, my relationship with God became clouded and the Lord seemed fearfully unreal and distant.

One Sunday Basil Gough preached on Col.3:15: 'Let the peace of Christ rule in your hearts.' He explained how the word 'rule' was used for the judge in the ancient Olympic Games who determined whether a competitor was running on the right track or whether he was cutting corners. A deep peace with God may signify that we are following the right course, but a consistent and lasting lack of such peace may be a sign that God wants us on a different track.

The tidal current of God's purposes was gently pushing me into new waters. I could not go on swimming against the current. The time had come for a definite decision to turn the direction of my life and accede to the Holy Spirit's promptings.

One morning before breakfast I was struggling to read my Bible and pray. The old gas fire in the little sitting-room of my mother's house warmed my hands, but my relationship with God seemed cool.

I was reading through the Psalms morning by morning and had come to Psalm 61.

'Hear my cry, O God, listen to my prayer; from the end of the earth I call to thee, when my heart is faint' (Ps.61:1–2). The voice of God seemed to speak so clearly from the Bible that morning. He would hear my cries to him 'from the end of the earth'. In the coming years my heart might indeed feel faint in the midst of all sorts of unknown trials, but God would listen to my prayer.

A strange mixture of anxious fear and yet of excitement came upon me as I quietly told the Lord that I would obey him and would serve him overseas as a missionary. But I knew so little about overseas mission. I thought you had to know right from the start which country God was calling you to, so I determined not to stop praying until God had made it clear which country I was to serve in. I had a very long time of prayer that morning! I don't think God wanted to tell me the country at that stage, but eventually I found my mind settling on the Philippines. After breakfast I rushed to the public Library to read up on the Philippines, for I knew so little about that land. In the coming weeks I discovered that the Overseas Missionary Fellowship worked in the Philippines and this led me into contact with the OMF.

As later chapters will show, under the wise guidance of OMF. leaders my course was directed away from the Philippines to other countries. We cannot force God to show us more than one step at a time. So I never worked in the Philippines, although I was to speak at conferences there in later years.

From this time on I knew that my future lay overseas in association with the OMF. Happily I had some years of preparation before me, so there was time to read widely about mission and about the work of OMF. I began to subscribe to the mission's magazine and to pray regularly for their work. I also knew that I needed more definite training for the work of mission to which God was calling me.

Training

A few years ago I broke one ankle and severely strained the other. What a relief it was to go to a highly qualified doctor and then to receive treatment later from a physiotherapist who used to work for a first division football side!

'If you were a footballer I'd get you back on the field in six weeks', he told me menacingly. 'But at your age it may take a little longer.' I felt total confidence in him and the results proved excellent.

We expect professional people to be properly trained, but sometimes we assume that Christians can serve cross-culturally overseas without relevant training. Often the result is that our practice of mission is distinctly amateur.

I knew that I needed training, so I went on from university to an Anglican theological college in Bristol. I revelled in the high quality of the Bible teaching, learning Greek and Hebrew with detailed study of some biblical texts in their original languages. Happily I was not pushed into taking any higher exam and so was free to follow my own desires in wider reading alongside the regular teaching courses of the college. The good library enthralled me and I devoured a range of biblical and theological books. Daily chapel times with their consecutive Bible readings according to the Anglican lectionary also fed my spirit. And we enjoyed rich fellowship together as students. All in all those years at theological college laid wonderful foundations and I learned so much.

But all the studies came from a very European

point of view. In those days, before Britain had welcomed large immigrant communities of other religious backgrounds, our theological college did not teach anything related to overseas mission or other faiths. The biblical studies and theology were also totally western and unrelated to cross-cultural mission. This meant that I had to do a lot of rethinking afterwards in order to adjust what I had learned to other cultural and religious backgrounds. Of course today the curriculum of such theological colleges has changed markedly to include considerable teaching on mission. But there may still be a danger that the biblical and theological studies will remain basically western.

While at theological college I faced a new opportunity to learn. We all were assigned to different weekend ministries and mine was with criminal teenagers in a senior approved school. In the navy I had related to the rough and tumble of life, so the segregated gentility of public school upbringing had already been shed. But now the challenge was how to relate to these lads in such a way that the good news of Jesus Christ could be meaningfully presented to them.

We worked together with a Christian couple whose home was open for the boys to visit at weekends. They were a wonderful couple who put all the comforts and possessions of their home at the disposal of these lads. The husband was a down-to-earth no-nonsense man while the wife's huge bulk towered over the boys with a loving discipline that brooked no nonsense. 'If you don't behave, I'll sit on you', she would declare — and such a dreadful fate would silence even the hardest criminal among them.

Communicating Christ in this context required new approaches to cross-cultural mission. This was excellent preparation for situations overseas which would be totally different but still definitely cross-cultural. I was learning to understand and relate to people from very different backgrounds from my own. And yet I soon found that even these youngsters with their long criminal records demonstrated beautiful sides to their natures. They were utterly loyal in their friendships; they were often wonderfully good fun to be with; they were so receptive to loving friendship. And if they came to faith in Christ they showed extreme courage in suffering fearful persecution for their new faith, often being beaten up by other lads.

While at theological college I also met the other end of the cultural spectrum.

'A missionary needs to be able to turn his hands to all forms of ministry', someone told me. By then I had had some experience with varying ages of adults, with students and with teenagers. But smaller children were an unknown quantity to me.

So I realized it would be useful to gain experience with children and learn something of how to work in that context. I therefore wrote to the most highly esteemed children's worker of those days in Britain and asked if I could come and learn at his feet. He kindly allowed me to work under him at a beach mission in Perranporth, Cornwall. He quickly threw me in at the deep end and asked me to speak in children's meetings, to lead games etc. He then told me in what ways I could have done it better. I learned a lot from him which came in very useful in future years both overseas and in Britain.

I have never become an expert in children's ministry and still avoid it if possible, but at least I learned to do the job competently when required. Since then I have often encouraged younger Christians to gain experience and help not only in the particular ministries to which they feel called and for which they feel gifted, but also to acquire some competence in other aspects of Christian work. It is good to be able to work with people of all ages and all social backgrounds.

Learning to preach

Soon after I came into the experience of new spiritual life at Oxford I was invited to preach in a church near my grandparents' home. It was an Anglican Church with quite a large congregation, so I was very nervous. I had never preached before and felt my knees knocking.

I climbed the stairs of the pulpit, settled my Bible and notes on the little reading desk with my watch in a prominent place to ensure that I kept to my time. I prayed with the congregation and began to preach.

As I settled into the sermon my hands went down to the wooden pulpit wall. Little did I know that it was rotten with woodworm! Suddenly the whole pulpit collapsed, leaving me standing with no covering protection on the plinth of the pulpit; my notes and Bible scattered below amongst the people in the front seats.

The whole situation was so traumatic I cannot now recall how I felt or what I did. Probably God helped me to complete the sermon, but I cannot honestly testify to that. Thus began my preaching career!

The vicar of my home church in Hove generously invited me each year from then on to preach on Maundy Thursday in our church. The congregation was of course smaller mid-week, but this experience helped me to gain more confidence in speaking publicly. I was always excited to see how people obviously found God spoke to them through these sermons and this encouraged me.

During one of our university vacations I joined a team holding an evangelistic week in the churches of Tunbridge Wells. One Sunday my turn came to preach. I was somewhat anxious not only because I was still quite inexperienced in preaching, but also because I had a bad sore throat and was in danger of losing my voice.

When the time came I duly mounted the pulpit steps and looked out onto the large congregation both in the main part of the church and also in the packed balcony. Everyone remained standing for prayer after the hymn and I opened my mouth to pray. Nothing came out except a hoarse whistle which circulated round the whole church through the PA system! I desperately drank some water, prayed very briefly indeed and descended into a fit of coughing.

A kind-hearted lad in the choir sneaked up the pulpit steps and handed me a bag of sweets which were obviously intended to entertain him and his friends during the tedium of my sermon. The sermon was reduced to a minimum with no extra adjectives or adverbs. Every sentence was punctuated with coughing. As the sermon came to an end I was ashamed. I knew it had been a disaster.

But after the service person after person came to me: 'Thank you so much for your preaching. God really spoke to me through what you said.' 'God called me this morning to commit myself to his service.' 'Until now my life has only been half-hearted for the Lord, but today God has spoken to me and now I'm determined really to live for him.'

To my amazement the Holy Spirit had used my weakness and the consequent pathetic sermon. Of course that does not excuse us from careful preparation, good communication skills and sensitively applied biblical preaching. But I learned in a new way the reality of God's overruling grace. His treasure is indeed in very earthen vessels and he uses us in our weakness and sin to bring glory to his name.

But I still had much to learn. Another lesson came in the months before I went overseas as a missionary. By then I had met and started to pursue Elizabeth, now my wife. She invited me to visit her home in Reigate as I was due to speak in a meeting near where she lived. Dressed in a suit ready for the evening meeting I walked on the heath with her. When we got home we saw the mud which had got onto my trousers and desperately tried to get them clean for the meeting.

On arrival at the church hall I got everything ready. I was due to show slides of Asia and needed to have the projector just right. As the people gathered I noticed with astonishment that nearly all of them were blind. They came from a local school for the blind — and I was showing slides! I realized too that a bit of mud on my trousers would not have mattered either!

In those early days of my Christian service it was not easy for me to be flexible and change everything. I really needed to laugh, cancel the showing of slides and just speak without visual aids. But I stumbled on with the slides.

This lesson of flexibility became of real importance later in a wide travelling ministry amongst all sorts of people of different racial, religious and cultural backgrounds.

It was in those early days too that I suffered my first experience of being stoned. Again it was as part of a team holding an evangelistic campaign in Toxteth, Liverpool. Every street held a pub on the corner. Each evening the gutters ran with drunken vomit and bodies lay in a stupor on the pavements. A large Irish community held strongly to a traditional Roman Catholicism of a pre-Vatican II type.

One day a small group of us were crossing a large open bomb site when a crowd of youths attacked us. Stones rained onto us most dangerously and several of us were hurt. Happily we were able to up-end one of the lads and use him as a human shield until the others ran away!

It was good for me to begin the process of learning that preaching the good news of Christ can sometimes lead to danger and suffering. The apostles experienced this in extreme measure, but I needed to experience the reality of suffering for Christ before going overseas into situations where my preaching might lead others into grave danger.

Marriage

Although languages were my delight and my university subject, I wanted all the training possible for the future task of learning an Asian language. I knew that good language learning is vitally important if we are to develop deep personal relationships overseas and communicate the good news of Jesus Christ effectively. So I signed up for an eleven-week course in linguistics and language learning.

The first evening all the new students were given badges on which we had to write our names and the mission we wanted to work with. Sporting these badges we all trooped into the evening meal. Opposite me sat a beautiful young woman, with blue eyes, light coloured hair, an intelligent forehead and an open smile. I fell in love at first sight and looked quickly at her badge to discover her name and whether she was heading for the same mission. Sure enough the badge clearly stated 'Elizabeth Hoyte — OMF' All was well and I began the pursuit.

While she soon learned to enjoy my company and friendship, she observed how immature I was. In addition I had no experience of girls and was singularly ham-fisted in any such relationship. I had grown up with no sisters, only two brothers; and then my schooling had all been single-sex. So Elizabeth ran a mile whenever I began to get too close.

But the chase was on! I sometimes wonder whether we qualify for the Guinness Book of Records for the number of countries in which I asked her to marry me and in which she said 'no'. It started in England, but the action moved to Egypt, Yemen, India, Sri Lanka, Malaysia — and finally we got engaged in Singapore. I asked her to marry me in each port en route from England to Singapore where we started our missionary career.

And what a delight the three-week sea journey was! We formed a group of thirty-five new missionaries together, playing deck games, swimming, reading and praying in the luxury and leisure of a P&O cruise ship. As we passed into the heat of the Red Sea we acclimatized in readiness for the steamy tropics of Singapore, but we could do so easily as we lazily consumed ice creams on deck and lounged on our deck chairs. Air travel today has enormous advantages, but we also miss much as we speed from continent to continent.

In 1960 television still lay in the future for most of us, so we had never seen pictures of the countries we passed through. We were fascinated by the sights and smells of Suez, Aden, Bombay, Colombo and Penang. So we began the process of being weaned from our own country and culture in preparation for settling into Asian life.

I revelled in the wonderful delight of sharing all these new experiences with someone I really loved, someone who right from our first meeting seemed to have the same mind and heart. But at the same time it was not easy to face her continued 'no'. I was so sure God wanted us together and I knew she was the one I loved and wanted to spend my life with, but despite her enjoyment of being together with me she did not yet love me and therefore could not give herself to me. In his generous grace God gave me various signs in answer to prayer to reassure me that I was on the right track.

Finally the day came when Elizabeth knew she loved me and we got engaged immediately. Our mission leaders kindly allowed us an afternoon off from our language studies and we enjoyed a beautiful stroll through the botanical gardens — all the orchids and other tropical flowers took on new colours that day and the royal palms seemed to salute us as we walked hand-in-hand between their dignified rows.

In those days our mission had strict rules about not getting married until after two years of language study and cultural adjustment, so we knew we had a long wait ahead of us. For seven months we were both in Singapore and could spend a good deal of time together. Then however, it became necessary for me to be transferred to South Thailand, hundreds of miles away from Singapore. Then after six months in Thailand I was granted my visa to enter Indonesia and moved to the land and work we felt God was really calling us to. But it meant long months apart with no access to telephones, and letters were slow and unreliable.

In her life-story *God can be trusted* Elizabeth has described more fully those months of separation and then the difficulties we had with visas for our wedding. For a while it seemed impossible for her to come across to join me in Indonesia or for me to come out to

Singapore, but God wonderfully helped me to get through the multitudinous offices and red tape to get out from Indonesia. We had fixed our wedding for Wednesday, 31 January; the visa was granted after many months of negotiation on Saturday, 27 January, but the offices were closed for the weekend. I raced to collect the visa on the Monday and then hurried to Garuda Airlines to try to book a flight to Singapore. There was just one flight before the wedding and I got the last seat!

What a relief to board that plane, land in Singapore and see Elizabeth there to meet me! She rushed me to the shops, the registry office for the civil marriage, the church to go through the order of service for the wedding and I don't know what else. Singapore seemed such a hectic busy place after the slower up-country life I had become accustomed to. While I had learned to do everything at a slower pace, Elizabeth was still living in the frenetic city life of modern Singapore. If we were not careful she was soon walking two paces ahead of me, dragging me after her — and she had finished her meals before I had hardly started. But what a thrill to be together again — and this time it was for good.

I went through the wedding as if in a trance. It was a different world from Indonesia — just the lavish spread of goodies at our reception overwhelmed me; nothing seemed real. But it was, and wonderfully so!

However, God had called us not only to the beauty of Christian marriage, but also to the privilege of serving him in mission.

Chapter 3

Singapore — First Lessons in Mission

Muslim evangelism

Although when we first arrived in Singapore our main task was to learn the Malay language, Muslim evangelism soon became a new and exciting expression of our mission passion. Two evenings a week I went out with a couple of more experienced workers to the night markets, displaying our Christian literature on a small stall and preaching over a loud-speaker. At first I could not preach because my language was quite inadequate, but I hovered at the edge of the small crowds distributing tracts and selling Gospels while trying to talk with people.

As is my custom when dealing cards, I handed out the tracts with my left hand. After some weeks I read in a book that the left hand is used only for the dirtiest of toilet purposes and therefore cannot be used in public without deep offence. The next evening I carefully changed and gave out the literature only with my right hand.

A smartly dressed Malay came up to me, took a piece of literature and in beautiful English said to me:

'I am glad to see you've learned some manners at least.'

He then walked away without further ado and left me to ponder his words. I realized that my cultural failure had ruined any testimony I thought I was giving. Instead of the gospel being something beautiful and attractive, I had made it something disgusting.

God was beginning to teach me the vital importance of cultural change, starting with rather obvious externals. Later I came to see that such adaptation would need to go much deeper than just the outward forms of acceptable behaviour.

There was so much to learn. I knew nothing about Islam, had never read the Qur'an and had not previously met Muslims' objections to the Christian faith. How does one communicate the gospel to Muslim friends? It was all new to me. My British theological training had not prepared me for the realities of pioneer Muslim evangelism. I began to read the Qur'an and books on Islam, to talk with Muslims and missionaries working in this field. I soon realized that I had begun a process of learning which would take a whole lifetime. But if the gospel was to be communicated in a loving, meaningful way such study was essential. Islam is a theological faith and as Christians we need to struggle with the questions Muslims put to us. But it is also a faith which is commonly mixed with all sorts of underlying folk religion. Superstitious traditional

beliefs and practices remain deeply embedded in the
daily life of many Muslims. Islam is also a proud faith
which confidently asserts that Muhammad is the final
prophet, the Qur'an is the supreme revelation from
God and Islam is the only final truth.

What a challenge Islam is to the Christian missionary! We can so easily feel terribly inadequate when first
witnessing to Muslims as new and inexperienced
workers.

Soon after I came to Singapore and started on this
life-time process of learning about Islam and relating
personally to Muslims, turmoil broke out in the Muslim community. In mass demonstrations abuse was
hurled at the followers of the Ahmadiyya sect, their
mosque was attacked and their well-known leader
suffered violence. But I had never heard of the Ahmadis
and did not know what all the fuss was about. One day
I was invited to visit the headquarters of the Singapore
Muslim Society, whose leaders I had come to know
through our open-air witness in the night markets.
When I arrived they were heatedly debating about the
Ahmadiyya movement. As they talked they banged
their fists on the table and I learned some new vocabulary which did not normally come into our somewhat
politer language course. Eventually they calmed down
sufficiently for me to be able to confess my ignorance
and ask them in what way the Ahmadis are heretical.
The contents of the Ahmadi Qur'an are arranged
slightly differently, they have different traditions of the
thoughts, words and deeds of Muhammad and they do
not spit out their melon pips in the same way as
Muhammad. So they informed me with further

vitriolic language. In my Christian theological studies the spitting out of melon pips had not played a very significant part and I was faced therefore with new questions. My witness was obviously not scratching where these people were itching. They were battling with issues which my gospel did not seem to touch at all. The struggle of communicating the good news of Jesus Christ to people of other faiths was beginning to impinge on my consciousness.

During that time I had the privilege of living and working with a much more experienced missionary. Sam Lewis patiently taught me so much about Islam and it was helpful to see how he related to local Muslim friends. He had created a badminton court in their garden, so each evening local Muslim men gathered in the relative cool of a tropical night to play badminton, drink orange squash and chat together. At the end of a day's work it was a pleasure to look forward to. And in the unthreatening context of flying shuttlecocks, dripping sweat and relaxed sipping of cool drinks friendships could naturally evolve.

Thus began a friendship which was to last for some ten years. Ahmed was a police sergeant and, like all the Malays, a Muslim. But he was curious to know about the Christian beliefs of Sam Lewis and myself. At first it was just a casual interest but gradually he came to see that in Christ lay truth. The more he examined the Christian message, the more deeply he became convinced that Jesus Christ could give hope for his Malay people. He was very aware that the Chinese dominated the Malays in Singapore because the Malays lacked the business-like diligence of their Chinese neighbours. He saw that Jesus Christ could change the whole character and outlook of his people. Jesus was not only the way to God the Father and the truth, but also the fulness of life for those who follow him.

'If you confidently believe that Jesus has the answers for yourself and for your people, you need to become a Christian', I said one day to Ahmed.

'Do you want me dead?' he immediately replied. 'If I became a Christian, I would be killed.'

I knew that Ahmed was not just being melodramatic, for Elizabeth and I had already observed the danger which Muslims may face if they become Christians. We had been asked to help a young Muslim student at the university in Singapore who had made a profession of faith in Christ. During her first vacation she had shared her faith with three sisters in her home village in Malaysia. These girls showed real interest and their mother became so concerned that she put poison in their tea and killed all three of them. Our friend was shattered and so were we.

So I knew that Ahmed's question was very serious. I could not give just a glib answer to my friend. I had to ask myself what Jesus really means to me; would I be willing to die for him? Is he more precious to me even than life?

Very seriously I replied after considerable thought, 'I would rather you were dead as a believer in Christ than alive without him.' Then I added, 'But I would rather you were alive as a believer in Christ.'

Sadly Ahmed shook his head. To this day he has never become a Christian. But I have had to ask myself whether I would have become a Christian if I had had to face martyrdom even before I had tasted anything of the beauty and glory of life in Christ.

The Malays seemed such easy-going and friendly people who loved peace and beauty. But violence lurked close beneath the surface and, if provoked, could erupt like a volcano.

One evening two other missionaries and I went as usual to the night market to distribute Christian literature and to preach. We set up our little stall alongside the many others with their bright lights and rich variety of goods for sale. The crowds sauntered along the street from one stall to another, enjoying the bustle of life and the relaxed atmosphere of a tropical evening. Then a growing number of Malays gathered around our stall to talk and buy books. Some among them did not like the fact that Muslims might be attracted to anything Christian, so they began to provoke trouble. Then they began to pelt us with stones and the situation turned nasty. My mind flashed back to the similar experience of being attacked with stones in Toxteth, but there was no time for reminiscing. We gathered up our things and ran in undignified haste to our car and escaped.

When working in another culture it is important to learn what may provoke people to volcanic anger. We pinned a Christian poster to the lamppost near our house. It pictured a set of scales with a bundle at either end. The small bundle at the light end was titled 'good works', while at the heavy end a large bundle read 'sins'. Beneath the picture ran the words from Daniel, 'you have been weighed in the balances and found wanting'. The poster was printed in the Malay language and clearly related to the Muslim belief that at the judgement we shall be weighed to see whether our sins or our good works prevail.

We soon learned how unwise we were! Riots broke out, the poster was ripped into little pieces, mob rule ran amok and peace could be restored only when the police moved in. We realized that less provocative methods of witness might be more appropriate in a Muslim context. The reality of future judgement lies sensitively close to the surface in many Muslim societies.

Our very direct evangelism among our Malay friends proved less effective than the slower, more gradual approach of quietly growing friendships.

We began also to consider whether it might prove more strategic to encourage the Chinese and Indian churches to catch the vision of witness among their Malay Muslim neighbours. Many local Christians lived and worked alongside Malays, but they had no interest in witness among them. They often lived an apartheid existence and there was considerable antipathy between the races. Ignorance of Islam and of Malay culture remained widespread among the Christians. But it dawned on us that mobilizing the church might prove more effective than trying to do the task of evangelism ourselves.

So we began to teach in some of the churches about Islam, Malay culture and our responsibility to share the good news of Jesus Christ with people of all races and religious backgrounds. Gradually the Holy Spirit stimulated this new vision in the hearts of some local Christians, and they began to witness very naturally to their Muslim neighbours. In the years since then God has called many local Christians to this work and it has yielded some fruit.

Back in the early 1960s when we began work among Malays in Singapore there was only a tiny handful of converted Muslims there. They belonged to different churches with the result that they had no fellowship with other Malay believers. So we decided to invite them to meet together one evening. Nine of them came, from Pentecostal, Anglican, Methodist, Lutheran, Independent and Brethren Churches. We sat in a circle and shared our testimonies of how we had become Christians.

It was fascinating to listen to their stories. What really struck me was that not one of them mentioned their conversion, but all of them stressed their baptism. I realized that persecution comes with baptism for a Malay believer; it does not come from mere faith in the heart. So the crunch comes with the decision to be baptized. The history of the European churches has caused us as evangelicals to struggle against a false doctrine of baptismal regeneration, but Muslim converts have a different history and face other issues. I was beginning to learn that we must not impose our western battles on overseas churches.

Work in local churches

Soon after our arrival in Singapore to begin our language study two Indian men came to visit me. Very graciously they invited me to come and preach in their

church. After some enquiries they informed me that
they belonged to the Mar Thoma Church. My church
history had not introduced me to this large Indian
denomination and I knew nothing about it.

I asked them what time their service began and they
told me that I should come at about midday and preach
for an hour. But they had not answered my question,
so I tried again.

'When does your service begin?'

'Come about midday and we should be glad if you
would preach for about an hour.'

It was stalemate!

Eventually I discovered that their service started at
about 9.30 a.m., but they told me that it was all in their
Malayali language. So they wanted to spare me the
tedium of sitting through long hours of a liturgy which
I could not understand. Nevertheless I determined to
arrive half an hour before they said in order to get a
feel of the church.

When I arrived, I immediately noticed the crowds.
With the main body of the church totally full, the
covered walk-way on three sides of the church was also
crowded with worshippers. The richly patterned saris
on the dark Indian skin added beauty and colour.

On my arrival some men ushered me to a seat near
the front where I could observe all the goings-on.
Priests and servers seemed to abound, each richly
dressed in vividly coloured and embroidered vestments. Incense wafted through the congregation in
large quantities. The leaders were constantly changing
vestments, bowing and crossing themselves repeatedly.
Servers bowed in humble service of the priests. The

chanting of the leaders was enthusiastically taken up by the large congregation. To my mind it seemed to make a Roman Catholic High Mass look as plain as a Brethren Breaking of Bread service.

I was bewildered because I had been told that this was an evangelical church with an active missionary vision. Certainly they drank in the Bible exposition I gave them that morning and listened in rapt attention.

Questions poured into my mind. Is colourful ritual necessarily associated with liberal theology or is that just an accident of western church history? Is incense unbiblical? Why does evangelical worship in the west lack symbolic ritual? Must we export our forms of worship overseas?

And why had my church history not taught me about these large Indian churches which were, according to tradition, founded by the apostle Thomas? Certainly they have a long history which antedates the arrival of western missionaries in India by many centuries. Is our teaching of church history biased, thinking that only European history has importance? Having worshipped in a Russian Orthodox Church for a while when at university I had become aware that western theology and church history books ignore the Orthodox Church, so it was not too much of a surprise to me to find that we had ignored other churches too. But what a privilege it proved to be when I was invited to preach fairly frequently in these Mar Thoma Churches during the ensuing years.

While at language school in Singapore Elizabeth and I had also the opportunity to build relationships with some of the Chinese churches. I started in the Anglican cathedral, but after a while an invitation came to teach an adult class in an independent church. This had been started by a dynamic missionary through whom many young Chinese came to faith. He had strongly taught them the vital importance of good Bible teaching, calling the preceding worship in the services 'the pre-liminaries'. The church leaders learned from him, stressing biblical teaching and subordinating every-thing else. Sunday services therefore began with one hymn and a brief prayer which was followed by almost an hour's solid biblical preaching. The service was preceded by an all-age Sunday School, in which all the church members received a good hour of Bible teach-ing! With his emphasis on Bible teaching the mission-ary had seemed to make worship and prayer insignificant. As so often happens, disciples exaggerate the emphasis of their teacher. So this new church practically omitted worship in their Sunday services. I realized that we need to be very careful what we teach a young church and what foundations we lay for the future development of a church.

Yet through this church we met many lovely Chris-tians and made good friends. Elizabeth had been born in China and lived there until she was eleven years old, but for me this was the beginning of a life-long rela-tionship with Chinese friends and their culture. Again I had so much to learn. I noticed however that my Jewish background related in some ways to Chinese culture and that helped me.

Many of these young adults came to our wedding. It was the first Christian wedding they had attended, so they observed everything with open eyes. Later an orphan girl in the church asked me to act as her father when she got married. Before their wedding they asked if they could come round to discuss the format of the wedding. They duly arrived at our home and produced a copy of our wedding service from their pocket.

'We want to have a modern Chinese wedding,' they affirmed, 'so could we go through your service order and what happened at your reception? Could we discuss what had a pagan background, what was truly Christian and what was just traditionally European?'

I was shocked, but also excited to work with them to pioneer new marriage forms for their church which would indeed be 'modern' and 'Chinese'. They were the first in their church to get married and their wedding formed the pattern for all future weddings in the group of churches which has grown out of that original congregation.

In those days the English-speaking Chinese churches in Singapore were all young people, for older folk had been educated in Chinese and did not speak English. It was a battle to encourage English-speaking Christians to remain steadfast in the church when they finished their studies and became immersed in the business world and the pressures of family life. But gradually the average age climbed in the churches and today they flourish with large congregations of all ages.

With their Confucian background the Chinese abound in dynamic energy and efficiency. These characteristics not only cause them to grow wealthy in business and to achieve notable success in the world of education, but their churches also flourish and grow. Strong and gifted leadership combines with great attention to detail in organization to give body to the spiritual vitality which flows in the Chinese churches. Our cultural backgrounds influence the whole development of the church.

The Chinese are proudly confident that they are a superior race. Their designation of China as the Middle Kingdom assumes that all other people are merely peripheral. Their civilization goes right back into the mists of pre-history and the Chinese were a cultured and educated people when the British were still living in caves and painting their bodies blue.

How important therefore that the Christian faith should have a properly indigenous Chinese image. Sadly we noticed in our early days in Singapore that western missionaries had exported their own forms of the church and the Christian faith with the result that most of the churches were just copies of a foreign model. Even today when the Chinese churches have become large and strongly independent with gifted national leadership, the forms and worship of the church remain quite western.

On one occasion I was invited to speak at the Christian Union in a college in Singapore. When I got out of my car I looked for someone from whom I could ask advice on how to find the particular lecture hall where the meeting was to be held. A young student kindly said he would show me the hall and he led the way.

'Are you a Christian?' I asked him after we had had some initial conversation. He replied rather firmly,

'No. I am Chinese. I couldn't be a Christian. I believe children should obey their parents.'

I thought of all those western missionary testimonies of how they had defied parental opposition in order to follow the Lord's call to mission. Is it biblical that youngsters should become independent of parental control at the age of eighteen or twenty-one? What does the Bible mean when it talks of 'honouring' parents?

The student's words came as a challenge. The gospel has to be clothed in Chinese fashion and shed its western image. We have to form patterns of family life which relate to Chinese culture and have firm biblical roots. We don't want lots of British or American books with their western teaching on family relationships.

Missionary travel agent?

As a young missionary it was a real help to work with and under older and more experienced workers who could guide and advise me. Later when I went to work in Indonesia I had to find my own way with the national church, but without the aid of more senior expatriate missionaries. What a blessing therefore to be able to start in Singapore with godly workers to oversee me!

One such did not belong to the mission agency I worked with, but he cooperated intimately with us. In fact he lived in Singapore as the sole representative of his denominational mission agency and so he was well-known to all from his churches who passed through Singapore en route from Australasia to Europe, and many Christians travelled that way. My poor friend seemed to be constantly in demand. So many people assumed that he would give them hospitality, show them the sights of Singapore and generally look after them when they passed through. Perhaps he should have been more rigorous in refusing to act as tour agent on their behalf, but it is not easy to be so hard-hearted. As it was, he reckoned to spend some three days a week looking after Christian tourists in this way.

In our day short-term mission has become the popular activity of young Christians and such short-term experience often proves to be the gateway into more useful long-term service. But it frequently happens that the few long-term workers spend much of their time and energy caring for and supervising the short-termers. We have to ask whether this is a good use of their time when they are the ones with knowledge of the language and culture. As long-termers they can relate deeply to local people, they have the respect of local churches and they can have a more effective ministry. It is sad if they are put in a position where all they can do is to look after young people who just come for a few months' wider experience. Mission agencies need to rethink the question of the care of short-term workers in such a way that the time of the key long-term missionaries is not wasted. Perhaps the answer is one or two senior workers who will go overseas specifically to look after short-termers; sometimes former missionaries could be called upon to fulfil this calling.

In my association with this more senior missionary it soon became obvious that he was receiving very considerable finance from his many friends overseas. The large number of Christians who met him when passing through Singapore gained an interest in his work and began to support him both in prayer and with money.

He was embarrassed at having so much money, for he remained a simple-hearted Christian worker for whom the things of this world held no great attraction. He therefore generously used his financial resources to pay for the literature and other activities we used in our evangelism among Malay Muslims. We all owed him a great debt, for our work could hardly have been continued without his help.

Happily in the OMF all workers received the same amount of money for our personal use, so there could be no jealousy between workers. This equality applied to us all whether we were top directors of the mission or just new workers. I observed how a more personalized support system may have many advantages, but it can lead also to great inequalities. My friend avoided this by his generosity, but not all missionaries show such unselfish wisdom.

Invest your life!

The Christian Union at Singapore University abounded, then as now, with vitality and spiritual fervour as well as attracting large numbers of students. It was a real privilege as a new missionary to be invited to speak at one of their weekly meetings and I prepared carefully and prayerfully.

After the meeting a young Tamil dentistry student approached me with the easy politeness born of his cultured background. I recognized immediately that Robert not only represented the best of the hard working and intelligent Singaporean student world, but also demonstrated a deep spirituality with a firm biblical grounding. I knew instinctively that this was the beginning of a life-long friendship.

Quietly Robert informed me that he and a small group of his friends were meeting regularly to pray about their lives after leaving university. Would I come and share with them one evening, he asked.

The other students who met with Robert were all Chinese, studying to become doctors, teachers or other white-collar professionals. I was impressed by the spiritual calibre and the mission potential of such high quality students. They gathered regularly with a map of Asia before them to pray about how God wanted them to invest their lives for his glory and for the spread of the gospel of Jesus Christ.

As they prayed, two questions were uppermost in their hearts. Firstly, they wanted God's guidance as to whether they should work in their professions or whether God was calling them to sacrifice this training and enter full-time Christian ministry. Secondly, they were asking the Lord where he wanted them to serve him. In what area of the map before them did God see a particular mission need which they could meet?

Some in wider mission circles might query why they had a map of Asia only in view rather than one of the whole world. It is true that as Christians we should share God's love not only for one part of the world, but for the whole world — 'God so loved *the world* that he gave his only begotten son . . .' (Jn.3:16). But at least a map of Asia was a good beginning. On that map live the majority of the world's population — China alone has as many people as Africa and Latin America together and India teems with a further nine hundred million people. Indonesia too has almost as many people as Britain, France and Germany together. So the map of Asia presented our friends with ample scope in which to fulfil a mission calling.

As they prayed, it became clear to them that God was calling them to use their professional gifts and training in his service. They were not to give these up in favour of working as pastors or full-time missionaries. They rightly believed that in their 'secular' professions they would equally fulfil a spiritual and missionary calling. In more recent years such thinking has become commonplace among evangelical Christians, but in those days in the early 1960s it sounded more radical. They, however, took it for granted without realizing that they were pioneering an approach to mission which would in the future become more usual.

The question of the geographical place still remained outstanding. Gradually their eyes focused on the east coast of peninsular Malaysia. In those days the small towns along that coastline formed the professional dustbin to which no-good failures were assigned by the government. It seemed like professional suicide to work there. But most of these little towns were largely unevangelized and they desperately needed good quality medical and educational services.

When they graduated, this little group of students scattered to different towns along the east coast to serve and to plant churches. Today there is a lovely

modern highway right up the coast and one can travel
speedily from place to place. As one goes to each town
it becomes clear that the church of Jesus Christ has
been planted — many of these churches issued from
the service of that little group of students.

My friend Robert went to one small town as a dentist.
As I know from personal experience, he performed his
dentistry in a gentle and loving manner. He took trouble
to spare his patients pain and distress. He was willing to
travel out to remote islands off the coast to bring modern
dental care to the little fishing villages there. He per-
suaded the government health department to provide him
with up-to-date equipment such as had not previously
been available on the remote east coast.

Robert's gracious manner, loving service and willingness to go the extra mile to help people opened
hearts to his quiet witness by spoken word. One by one
Chinese and Indian people began to believe in Jesus
Christ and an English-speaking church started with
Robert as its leader. Later when I pastored a church in
Malaysia it was my great privilege to preach in that
church once a month. This afforded us a short holiday
too, for the east coast of Malaysia is very beautiful with
wonderful facilities for swimming. And Robert's hospitality always warmed the heart as well as cosseting
the body.

Despite his willingness to sacrifice professionally
Robert now has a thriving practice and he has even
been honoured for his service to leading people in
society as well as to many ordinary people. God is
nobody's debtor and in one way or another rewards
those who sacrifice themselves in his service.

Chapter 4

South Thailand — Getting Stuck In

After much prayer and discussion our mission leaders had designated Elizabeth and myself to work in Indonesia, but in those days visas for Indonesia often got bogged down in the morass of bureaucracy. It was common to have to wait several years for a visa. Some workers waited impatiently with their eyes fixed on the goal of Indonesia, but failed to contribute positively to the work in the country where they sat out the years of waiting. I firmly believed that if God allowed me to live and work somewhere, it was my responsibility to commit myself fully to the life and work of that country. Then I could refocus my attention on Indonesia when the visa eventually came.

After almost a year in Singapore the mission leaders asked me to join the team in South Thailand to work among Malay Muslims there. Although the majority population was of the same Malay race as those in

Singapore, their dialect was radically distinct, even to the extent of needing a different translation of the Bible.

When studying at Oxford I had much enjoyed the literature and language studies as well as my further study in Russian political thought, but I had rebelled against the study of the old Church Slavonic which is the Russian equivalent to Anglo-Saxon English. We had also to work on the history of the development of slavonic languages over the centuries and how they evolved. Having reacted against these apparently useless studies I now found them really helpful, for they enabled me to understand how the various dialects of Malay evolved and thus to learn the South Thailand dialect quite quickly.

God's overall plan for our lives often includes those elements which we at first think useless and against which we are tempted to rebel. He often weaves into the stuff of our lives all the little threads of our earlier training and development. We never know what will become significant and valuable later in life.

But I was still struggling at an early stage of language learning as my first year in Asia came to its close. Again I had the privilege of working under an experienced missionary. Mac Bradshaw was a dynamic American with unbounded enthusiasm. I remember a team of us setting out by bus for an evangelistic outreach in a Muslim village. On arrival we rented an empty house by the river where we slept on the floor and could receive visitors as well as using the house as our base. The toilet consisted of a hole in the wooden balcony over the river. When one used the toilet it attracted a multitude of richly coloured tropical fish and sea snakes, so that a visit to the toilet resembled a visit to a beautiful aquarium.*

In the afternoons we cycled through the rice fields from village to village with a loudspeaker perilously held in one hand. Crowds of children followed us as we sang Malay translations of songs like 'Jesus loves me, this I know' and advertised the evening meetings.

'Come — and see the fantastic film showing of the great prophet Noah and the flood.'

In the evening we planned to show an old film strip about Noah, but we lacked equipment. One of my fellow workers had tremendous practical skills and he converted a large torch into a small projector. For a screen we had a big white sheet. We asked the villagers where we could pin the sheet and some youngsters pointed to a house in the centre of the village. The door and windows were all closed and it was evidently not occupied, so we duly pinned the sheet over the front of the house covering the door also.

The crowds gathered in the area in front of the house and we sensed the excited expectancy of the young people particularly. Finally all was ready; about five hundred people were present.

To our horror we noticed a movement behind the sheet. The door of the house half opened and then the head of an old woman poked round the end of the sheet to be greeted with loud applause and laughter. Finally we did show our film strip, sang some lively songs and preached.

*My wife insisted on me adding this detail!

Later I read a report of this evangelistic outreach in our mission magazine. Mac wrote how from the moment we got on the bus we had been carried along in victory by the gracious power of the Holy Spirit. His enthusiasm went beyond my recollection of it!

But Mac was always enthusiastic and felt confident that God was at work. As a result he was the only one among us who actually did see people coming to faith in Christ. At that time in South Thailand no Malay had been converted, but Mac had the joy of leading two men to the Lord. I learned the significance of positive enthusiasm.

Mac helped me in another way also. He was holding the rapt attention of a crowd of about a thousand Muslims with his dynamic preaching when suddenly to my horror he announced, 'We have here today with us Martin Goldsmith who will now speak.'

With no preparation and in my still far from perfect Malay I began to speak. When finally I stopped and the crowd was still listening, Mac grinned and exclaimed, 'You held them. That was great.'

I admired his courage in trusting me to speak with such a large crowd and also his desire to encourage a younger worker to develop as a speaker. How easy it would have been for him to continue speaking while the crowd thronged around and then let me speak when they had largely drifted away!

Hospital Evangelism

My main work was as evangelist at the OMF's mission hospital at Saiburi. This little hospital nestled in the sands near the east coast just outside a pretty little fishing port. Evening strolls by the harbour and glorious swimming opportunities provided delightful relaxation after the hot days. But the work lay heavily upon us in this pioneering situation.

Each morning I joined the out patients for about four hours as they waited to see the doctors. I tried to share the gospel personally with each of the hundred or so patients, talking with them and telling Bible stories with the aid of colourful pictures. During the morning we also held a short evangelistic service in each ward and it was often my responsibility to lead and preach briefly. Then in the afternoons after a short siesta I wandered down to the wards and talked with the in-patients and their families until the evening meal. Most of the Malays knew nothing at all about the Christian faith and it meant beginning from scratch. If nothing else was happening, the evenings were dedicated to further language study and preparation of talks.

Every day I met quietly for prayer with one of the doctors and with Minka Hanskamp who was the evangelist for the local Thai people. Later she and a younger worker were kidnapped by local rebels up in the jungle-clad hills and held to ransom. When OMF followed the policy of not giving in to ransom demands, they were murdered. Minka was a fine Christian woman and their martyrdom shocked us all.

Each week I looked forward to Friday, the Muslim day of prayer. Then I would have a break from the regular work in the hospital in order to take the gospel more widely into the villages. Through the hospital I had contacts wherever I went, so this gave me a natural opportunity for visiting the many villages around Saiburi to preach and teach further about Jesus Christ. It was hot work cycling from village to village in the burning heat of the tropical sun and by the end of a ten- or twelve-hour day a long cool drink and a cold shower seemed greater luxuries than any Hilton hotel could have offered. For my lunch I would stop at a local food stall and order a plate of fried rice or whatever local food was available.

Sometimes on a Friday I treated myself to a special delight. I would leave my cycle at home and travel by little boats from village to village up one of the rivers. What a pleasure to sit with local people on these boats and share Jesus Christ with them until we got to the next village. Then I would get off the boat, visit people and preach for a while before finding another boat on to the next village.

The hospital had such a good reputation and people were so grateful for the loving care they received there that I was always welcome wherever I went. In those days Muslims in South Thailand were by no means fanatical, so they were happy to hear the Christian message. Thailand boasted complete religious freedom, so there were no restrictions on the followers of any faith preaching and teaching what they believed.

The local culture even allowed me as a man to speak with women and share the gospel with them. Of course it was important to learn how a man should relate to a woman without appearing immoral or conveying the wrong message.

I learned the dangers of not observing the cultural

limits very early in my time at Saiburi. When cycling out from the hospital each Friday morning I used to greet the middle-aged wife of the leader of the Christian church in the town. She worked in the hospital laundry and came to work each morning along the path which I used to cycle out from the hospital. So our paths crossed once a week and I would cheerfully say 'good morning' in my best Thai language — almost the only words I knew in Thai and she spoke no Malay.

After some weeks I was summoned by the hospital superintendent because this lady had complained that I was flirting with her and wanting a sexual relationship with her. I was of course happily engaged to Elizabeth at the time and had no intentions at all with this Thai lady with greying hair who was old enough to be my mother and bulged in all the wrong directions! But I had looked at her face for a brief moment when saying 'good morning' and that was not acceptable. Cross-cultural workers have to learn how to behave with people of the other sex — it is important.

Nevertheless if I was culturally careful it was possible to talk with local women about Christ as well as with the men. For example I remember one day meeting a Malay lady and sharing the gospel with her. Knowing that she had a dozen or so children, I asked her how she felt about the Muslim teaching that children are morally responsible for their sin only when they are twelve years old. Only at twelve can they really chose between right and wrong.

Without a moment's hesitation she replied sweetly: 'My dear, theology is for men'! In a chauvinistic society what more could one say! I could only laugh with her.

In such pioneer Muslim evangelism it was easy to become discouraged and even to lose hope of seeing any positive response to one's work. Thus I remember going to preach in one village and a small crowd gathered to listen to what I had to say. After a while a man at the back of the crowd called out,

'That's right. I believe that. What he says is truth.'

The thought ran through my mind that the man was probably mentally troubled and not in his right mind, so I continued to preach and ignored his exclamation. In fact I never made the effort to talk with this particular person after I had finished, so I don't know even now what prompted his words. Very likely I was right and he did not understand the significance of what he said, but it could be that I missed the opportunity of leading someone to faith in Christ. It is said that those who aim at nothing will hit nothing. If we do not expect results, we shall not get results.

When my visa came for Indonesia I had prayed and worked hard for six months together with the whole team of other OMF workers, but we had seen no fruit for our labours at all. Not one single person had come to faith in Jesus Christ.

Twenty years later I returned with my wife and youngest daughter to revisit South Thailand and show them the places where I had previously worked. On one occasion I heard a loud call: 'Yusuf!' I paid no attention, not thinking it had anything to do with me. I had forgotten after twenty years that my Malay name in South Thailand was 'Yusuf'.

A man came running to us and introduced himself

to us. He informed us that he was now a leading Christian in the little congregation of converted Malays in Saiburi and that he had first heard the gospel when I had preached in the open air in his village one Friday.

In reading the history of Christian mission more recently I have come to realize that many missionaries do not see fruit from their work until many years later — and some never see it except if they look down from heaven after their death. Many of the major movements of church growth around the world have started with the persevering faithfulness of a Christian worker who has never seen any results during his or her life-time. Perhaps that is God's purpose so that we do not take the glory to ourselves, but learn to work for his name's sake alone. However, it was encouraging after those twenty years to find that there had been some fruit after all.

What a joy it was also to have the opportunity on this visit to speak to the small Christian gathering in Saiburi on the Sunday. There were just sixteen local believers, of whom fifteen were people who had been treated for leprosy at the hospital. Most of them carried the deformities which so often accompany this dreadful disease — distorted mouths, misshapen ears, missing noses, fingers and toes. But the light of Christ lit their faces.

As we gathered, the Christians sat facing in different directions with no sense of dignity or order. None of them had bothered to change their clothes for worship or wash their hands. It was all very casual and lacking the sense of awe which a Muslim would expect when coming to worship Almighty God in his majestic splendour. Casual informality in worship may suit the modern culture of Europe, but it proves a scandal and a stumbling-block in a Muslim society. So I felt it right to encourage them gently to smarten up their style of worship and trust that they will have followed that advice. Otherwise they will not be able to attract Muslims of quality to their Christian gatherings.

Despite the encouragement of seeing that our work back in the early 1960s had after all yielded some fruit, it has still to be said that the harvest has not proved bountiful. After several decades of hard work only small struggling fellowships have emerged, no large or dynamic churches. Scattered around the whole area perhaps as many as a hundred ex-Muslims now believe in Jesus Christ, but few of them show strong evidence of their faith.

Missionaries have not found it easy to endure with perseverance the discouragement of such hard and apparently fruitless ministry. Over the years the turnover of mission personnel has been high and this militates against effective witness in the area. New missionaries have to spend years learning the language and adapting to the culture as well as gaining some experience in communicating the gospel to South Thailand Muslims. Happily some missionaries have faithfully remained and they have become the key workers who can also guide the newer folk.

We who live in western societies today expect things to happen speedily. When speaking in Scandinavia or continental Europe I sometimes say that our modern culture has moved from the era of filter coffee to instant brews. Percolated coffee drips so slowly through the filter and is indeed a most inefficient method of making coffee, for it wastes precious time. Instant coffee is much more efficient. But we all know that Nescafé cannot match the fragrance or taste of proper percolated coffee. So it is with Christian mission among Muslims. It demands patient endurance which sees the long-term potential of our ministry. Those who insist on immediate results will quickly feel that their work lies outside the blessing of the Holy Spirit and will therefore give up and return to their home country. We see this happening with frightening frequency in all Muslim countries. Christian workers among Muslims need much prayer and positive encouragement. Sadly many of us prefer to support work that shows exciting fruitfulness and have not the patience to 'continue steadfastly in prayer' (Col.4:2) for those who labour in unresponsive situations.

In South Thailand I noticed too how many of our workers seemed to lack any overall sense of strategic purpose and so could not see how their daily activities fitted into the pattern of what God was doing in the area. I came to see the important role Christian leaders can have in this respect. They need of course to be good administrators and have pastoral skills. But we also require some of our leadership to have gifts of encouragement and inspiration together with the ability to see the overall strategic purpose and plan of the work. This then needs to be carefully imparted to each worker in the team. While these principles of leadership apply particularly to those working in Muslim contexts, I believe they have significance for all leadership teams in any situation.

It has to be said however that I personally faced other problems when I lived in South Thailand. In the whole team of expatriate workers in our mission hospital I was the only single man. There were many single women and married couples, but being a single man could prove quite lonely. If I formed friendships with the single women and spent time with them, gossip began to circulate both among the expatriates and also among local people. The married couples were warmly welcoming and I had most of my meals in the home of a loving family with two delightful children, but I sometimes felt they needed time on their own as a family in the midst of a busy and pressurized life. I did not want to outstay my welcome and intrude too much on their time. The only local single man of my age in the hospital team was Thai and he spoke no Malay, so we could not communicate beyond the occasional exchange of smiles.

Nevertheless we did have good times. Occasionally someone organized a picnic after work on the beach when we all gathered for a swim and a happy time in the cool evening as the sun sank behind the palms fringing the beach. I looked forward too to those days of outreach when a whole team of us would go to some village for a few days of evangelism and worked closely together in this.

I have happy memories also of my meals with the more senior couple and their children. On one occasion we were sitting comfortably after breakfast having prayer and a good chat together. Then we became aware that the children seemed very quiet and we did not know where they were or what they were doing. Their mother went to investigate and then called us urgently. The two small children were in the bathroom playing with two large scorpions. They were poking the scorpions' backs with their fingers and watching the tails with the stings snapping at them while they hurriedly pulled their fingers away. If the scorpions had succeeded in stinging them the children could have died from the shock of the pain. Such shared dangers help to bring Christians closer together in a deep way.

Another of my difficulties related to the local church. The small group of ex-Buddhist Thai Christians met in a shop-front house in the town. I did not attend their services because they were conducted in Thai and I spoke only Malay. But after some weeks people began to complain that the missionary's testimony was not good because I was not seen to share in worship with other Christians. It was therefore strongly suggested that on Sundays I should attend the church. Week by week after that I had to sit through their long services without understanding a word. Even the songs followed a Thai meter which was so utterly different from English music that I found it impossible to follow the singing. For them it was wonderful because they loved their traditional music style and a well-known Christian ex-actor had written many beautiful Thai hymns. But for me it was difficult. The small benches had no backs and after an hour or two they seemed fearfully uncomfortable in the stifling heat of a crowded room on a tropical day. Evangelizing in the hospital, preaching in the villages, taking boats up the rivers, sharing in beautiful picnics by the seaside — that was all quite enjoyable, but those long hours in the church seemed interminable. I tried to discipline myself to pray for each person in the church in turn; my mind wandered round the different villages where I was preaching the gospel; friends and family swam into my numbed consciousness and more prayer ensued; and often my mind rested romantically with Elizabeth down in Singapore and I dreamed of our times together.

Since those days I have often had to sit through all sorts of Christian services and meetings in languages which I have not understood, so my experience in South Thailand has proved useful. I have learned to switch off and dream as well as to pray. The danger is sometimes in dreaming too much and praying too little!

In so many ways my brief six months in South Thailand were formative in my mission experience with a host of new lessons to be learned.

The spirit world

Before moving to Saiburi I lived for a while in Sungei Golok, a thriving market town on the river which forms the border between Thailand and Malaysia. While a tiny group of four or five Chinese Christians hesitatingly reflected the light of Christ, generally Satan's darkness ruled almost unchallenged. Poisonous snakes glided dangerously into unexpected places, rats scuttled along the rafters of my dark upstairs bedroom, a steady stream of smugglers brazenly forded the river and walked past our house with contraband goods on their shoulders.

The local imam not only led the Muslim community

of the town, but also headed up all criminal activities — smuggling, theft, prostitution and drug dealing all came under his control.

One day another missionary had his bicycle stolen. We went to visit the imam to tell him what had happened and ask for his help. While his eyes remained firmly dark, his hard face lit up with a smile of apology.

'I'm so sorry', he said, 'I'm sure the man who took it did not realize it belonged to you. It will be returned.'

Sure enough, that afternoon the bicycle mysteriously found its way back to our house and we found it casually placed, leaning against the outside wall.

That evening I thanked God again for the biblical emphasis that religion and ethics must always go inseparably hand in hand. The biblical God reveals himself as absolutely holy and pure. He then commands his people also to be holy even as he is holy.

While at Sungei Golok I had my first encounter with the realities of the spirit world in Islam. I was quietly reading in my bedroom after a long day of language study and evangelism when the night silence was shattered with the loud beat of drums, frenzied music and intermittent shouting. It came from a Malay home behind our house, so we went out to see what was happening.

A large crowd had assembled to watch a 'bomoh', a Muslim spirit medium, in action. He was attempting to heal a young lad who was seriously ill. This particular 'bomoh' was known as the 'revolving bomoh'. To the heady accompaniment of the music he would go slowly down onto his haunches and then slowly up again. All the time while doing this he whirled his head round and round, causing his waist-long hair to whirl loose like a propellor. His hair revolved so fast that it was impossible to see just where it was — just as you cannot tell the exact position of a propellor's blades.

When I got home that evening I went to my bedroom with questions racing through my mind. I stood before the mirror and tried to revolve my head as the bomoh did, wondering just what is humanly possible without the aid of spirits. Of course my hair was somewhat shorter than his! But still I soon realized that I could never make my head go round at that speed.

A few days later the whole performance was repeated; the boy was still seriously ill. This time we did not watch, but quietly prayed at home. Not long after the second evening with the revolving bomoh the boy died.

Later in Saiburi I came to know another bomoh, this time one who was known as the 'fish bomoh'. I had heard of his powers and was curious to see whether he was as powerful as people said. He kindly invited me to go out on a fishing trip with him. Praying for Christ's protection I agreed to go.

About a dozen fishing boats gathered under his command. Their brightly painted sides with various occult designs made the little fleet a romantic sight as we all set off into the ocean with our outboard engines whirring expectantly. Suddenly when we were right out at sea my bomoh friend ordered the boats to stop their engines. Silence reigned. The bomoh dipped his head into the water and remained submerged for what seemed an impossibly long time. Then he took his head out of the water.

'There is a large shoal of fish moving in that direction.' His arm pointed further out to sea. He informed us what sort of fish they were, what speed they were travelling at and told us they were about three or four miles away from us. He duly organized us so that we could cut the fish off. We formed a long line at the designated place, let down our nets between the boats and hauled in the fish. It was a large catch of the type of fish he had told us.

We know that fish do make a noise as they swim, but is it possible for the naked human ear to catch their sound at such a distance? I doubt it. I did not question that the bomoh was exercising supernatural powers — and this was not the work of the Holy Spirit, but of some demonic spirit.

Over the past thirty years I have visited Christian workers in many Muslim countries and I have no doubt that superstitious folk Islam allows demonic powers to gain control. I have observed how even normally bold Christians often seem paralysed in their witness by a spirit of fear. I am not the sort of person who commonly uses the expression 'a spirit of . . .' For example, I don't believe most of us have a spirit of laziness that needs exorcism. Normally we are just lazy. The answer lies not in casting out a demon of laziness, but in buying an alarm clock and exercising more self-discipline!

I am convinced that in the world of Islam we are dealing not only with a theological system, but also with demonic spirits which have very real power. Christians working in the Muslim world need therefore to cover themselves with the righteousness and power of Christ through prayer. It gives us a quiet assurance when we can rest in the great truth that as Christians we live 'in Christ', covered on all sides by him. Only then can we effectively counter the spirits' power.

Group movements

Over a period of time I became quite friendly with a middle-aged Malay man who came each week to the hospital for treatment. Week by week I shared different aspects of the Christian message with him and he particularly enjoyed the Bible stories about Jesus.

'Why don't you come to our village and share lunch with us?' he asked me. 'I would love you to tell those stories about Jesus to the others in the village.'

He told me the name of his village and very roughly where it was. We arranged that I would bicycle out on the following Friday. When I asked the other hospital workers, no one had ever heard of this particular village. Someone lent me an ordinance survey map. In the approximate locality of the village the map showed a large green square with the word 'unexplored' on it. Very helpful!

I set off early that Friday and started down the little dirt road as he had told me. At each village I came to I asked for directions. Using their chin to point they encouraged me to proceed further down the road. Gradually the dirt road degenerated into a rough track and cycling became hard going — and the tropical sun climbed higher, beating unmercifully on my head. At each village I wrote down its name as best I could and noted the distance by cycle from the previous village. When the path forked, I noted that too so that others might follow after me to preach in these places. Finally after some four hours of hard pedalling I reached the village. It was right at the end of the track with nothing but virgin jungle beyond.

My friend welcomed me warmly, his wife served me with lunch and they then called all two hundred of the village's inhabitants to gather around me to listen to my preaching. It turned out that my friend was the headman and all the villagers were related to him. He was the patriarch with considerable authority over them all.

I preached and answered questions in discussion for a couple of hours and then made my weary way home. I knew that I had certainly pushed back the frontiers of pioneer mission, witnessing to Christ where no other Christian had ever been. But I did not realize the real significance of this remote little village — and none of my fellow-missionaries did either. We all had much to learn.

With everyone in the village being related to each other and under the authority of my friend the headman, there could have been a real possibility of the whole village turning together in a group movement to Christ. The village had no mosque and no Muslim leader to put pressure on them. I should have gone back to that village again and again to foster their interest and teach. However, I thought of it as just one more tiny village in a remote area. There were hundreds of unevangelized villages around, many of them bigger and more influential than this one. But here I did have the opportunity of a whole village turning to Christ and then becoming the base for further outreach back down the mud path to other villages.

It was only when I reached Indonesia that I realized my error and saw the reality of whole groups turning to Christ together. In a Muslim context persecution of converts can be so fierce that it becomes almost impossible for a lone individual openly to declare faith in Christ and be baptized. But if a whole village turns together . . .

Holistic medicine

'We're facing a problem', the medical superintendent of Saiburi hospital told me when I revisited there. 'Local Muslims are openly saying that our missionary doctors excel in dealing with viruses and other physical problems, but they don't know how to deal with the spirit world. Local bomohs, on the other hand, are brilliant in relationship to the spirits, but are ignorant about the physical side of illness. Add a visit to the bomoh to hospital treatment and you get good medicine!'

I realized the dangers of western atheism influencing all our professions. In reaction to the medical profession which touches only the physical and emotional sides of illness some Christians emphasize miraculous healing which uses only spiritual means. But God remains head over every side of our lives.

So I suggested a more holistic approach to the treatment of patients at Saiburi. The doctors should lay hands on every patient and pray with them that God would use the treatment given to bring relief from their trouble.

'But that will take so much time. We won't be able to see so many patients each morning', a doctor objected. I pointed out that we can't see everyone who is ill anyway, so we're not fundamentally changing the situation. And it may be better to give holistic treatment to a slightly reduced number of people rather than helping more people physically, but unconsciously declaring that illness is only a physical problem and 'we don't handle spiritual battles!'

Later when I worked in Malaysia the same question emerged again but in relationship to education. In our neighbouring town a young American Christian came with the Peace Corps to teach in a large secondary school. He attended the local evangelical Methodist church, but they never asked him to have any ministry among them. He became a little frustrated as he longed to serve and had obvious gifts.

One day two young leaders from that church came to my house to invite me to speak at their meeting. I told them that sadly I was unable to accept for that date and suggested they invite our American friend. They clearly had no intention of doing so and I enquired why.

'We don't normally invite atheists to minister in our church', they eventually replied.

'But he's not an atheist. He is a committed Christian. You know that; he prays fervently in your prayer meetings and is keenly involved in your church.'

They insisted that he was an atheist. They had no

doubts and reminded me that he worked in their town and they knew him better than I did.

When I asked them what gave them the impression that he was an atheist, they replied,

'He has taught physics in our school for a whole year and has never once mentioned God in class. How can you teach physics without talking of God if you are a Christian? The whole of science depends on the reality of order which God has created in the world.'

I had to explain to them that Christians in the west have been pressurized by our secular society so that it has become almost unacceptable to mention God in the classroom. Secular atheism has prevailed in the world of education.

But many societies overseas have not developed this dichotomy between the secular and the spiritual. Our whole approach to education, medicine, agriculture and other professions has to be rethought.

Chapter 5

Indonesia — Mass Movement and Large Churches

The background

What a radical change! After a wonderful holiday with Elizabeth in the cool mountains of Malaysia and the welcoming holiday bungalow of the OMF, the plane transferred me from South Thailand to North Sumatra, Indonesia, from the pioneer situation of Muslim evangelism to a land with huge fast-growing indigenous churches. In South Thailand the gospel of Jesus Christ was still quite new to most of the Muslim population, whereas in North Sumatra most people knew some basic Christian truths and biblical stories. The history of the church in Indonesia stretches back through the centuries.

I sometimes smile when I read in western books that

Carey was the father of modern mission in the last decade of the eighteenth century. Of course the Moravians and other non-English speaking missionaries had already been active in spreading the Christian faith to other countries, but the Dutch colonialists also had planted large Indonesian churches.

Back in the fifteenth and sixteenth centuries Roman Catholic missionaries had spread the Christian faith in the spice islands in the east of Indonesia. Great men like Francis Xavier had laboured in those parts with considerable results. Latourette says in '*A History of Christianity*' (Eyre and Spottiswoode, 1954) that by 1569 the Jesuits were 'in charge of eighty thousand Christians'. But then towards the close of the sixteenth century the Dutch through their East India Company wrested control of that part of the world. With the principle of '*cuius regio eius religio*' (those who have power determine the religion) the Dutch Reformed Church became the established church of the region. According to Stephen Neill (*A history of Christian Missions, Penguin, 1964*) the Dutch claimed 100,000 Christians in Java and 40,000 in Ambon by the end of the seventeenth century. In 1668 the New Testament was published in Malay, the first translation of the Bible in South-East Asia.

Soon after my arrival in Indonesia in 1961 I had the great privilege of being invited to preach at a celebration of the centenary of the founding of the great Batak church by the well-known German missionary Ludwig

Nommensen. Today Batak Christians can be numbered in their millions and they represent a significant force in the church of Indonesia. We were called to work in the ethnic church of a smaller Batak race known as the Karo Batak people. Evangelism began among them some twenty-five years later than with the main Batak people and when we arrived in North Sumatra there were only about 20,000 Christians out of a total Karo Batak population of 300,000. They were therefore a tiny part of the total Indonesian church which at that time numbered about five million Christians. The population of Indonesia was then about a hundred million.

Since then the Indonesian population has doubled to about two hundred million, the fourth largest nation in the world after China, India and the USA. The church too has multiplied, but it is impossible to give any accurate statistics as those quoted are consistently understated. It is said that between 1965–1968 the church grew from five million to somewhere between twelve and fifteen million. Since then it has also continued to grow quite significantly.

Our Karo Batak church which had only about 20,000 members in 1961 had grown to 25,000 by the time we left Indonesia in 1964 and then multiplied further to about 75,000 or 80,000 by 1968. Since then it has added each year to its numbers and now stands at about 250,000–300,000 members out of a total Karo Batak population of some 600,000. It was into this staggering situation of growth that God was calling us to minister.

OMF in Indonesia

The China Inland Mission, the precursor to the OMF, was founded in 1865 as a pioneer church planting mission to the unreached areas of inland China. When Chairman Mao gained power in China the Communist government forced all missionaries to leave the country. The CIM surveyed the countries around China to see what church planting needs might be found to which their workers could be redeployed.

Although there were already large churches in many parts of Indonesia, the mission felt called to a solidly Muslim people in West Sumatra, the Minangkerbau. When I became interested in the OMF. I remember reading many articles about the Minangkerbau in *The Millions*, the mission's magazine. We were informed about this people and their needs. And we were urged to pray that OMF workers might gain entry into that area in order to fulfil this evangelistic calling.

But Indonesia had its own laws concerning foreign workers. We had to be sponsored by an existing Indonesian body to work within their organization. The mosques among the Minangkerbau showed little interest in sponsoring OMF missionaries to evangelize in their midst! As a result the mission was forced to accept church sponsorships for work in the already existing churches. So it was that we were invited to Indonesia by the Karo Batak church to serve in their midst and under their leadership.

Sometimes I hear mission propaganda which denigrates missionaries who are involved in church work as opposed to pioneer evangelism and church planting. Such workers are accused of merely maintaining the status quo and not serving at the cutting edge of mission for the sake of those who have never heard the gospel. The OMF's experience in Indonesia is that we have been enormously fruitful through mobilizing Indonesian Christians, so that it is they who do the work of evangelism in their own country. Of course they get the glory because it is they who have planted churches and fulfilled God's calling to evangelism. This indirect method of church planting through bringing vision and teaching to existing churches has proved much more fruitful than when we as foreigners have tried to do the work ourselves.

In post-colonial Indonesia, as indeed in many Asian contexts, the greatest stumbling-block for the gospel of Christ is that it is often considered a foreign faith which is alien to local people. Happily we found in North Sumatra that we could take a back seat and local Karo Batak Christians stood in the limelight. The public image of the church remained Indonesian rather than becoming foreign.

So it was that the Karo Batak church invited the OMF to lend them a missionary couple to serve with them. In the former colonial days they had suffered missionary domination and they were determined that never again would they have foreigners lording it over them. In the past only Dutch missionaries had been ordained as ministers in the Karo Batak church and almost all the church finances had come from Holland — and money always tends to have strings of power attached.

With these things in mind the church laid down four conditions for our coming:

1. We were not to bring any foreign finance into the church. We were allowed to give an offering on a Sunday, but it should not be more than an ordinary teacher would give — and we found that this was very little indeed. This prevented us gaining influence through our money.

2. We were to live in the house that the church gave us. We could not choose for ourselves at what level we wanted to live. In this way they ensured that we live at their level and not in the old colonial manner. They gave us a simple wooden house in a row of shop-front houses without a garden. We had just one room upstairs and one downstairs with a hole in the ground at the back for the toilet. There was no kitchen, but we put our kerosene stove under the outdoor staircase. We had no running water and no electricity. But local people felt at home there and we had a constant stream of visitors which was ideal for the mission we were called to.

3. We were not allowed to open our mouth in any church meeting whether administrative or 'spiritual'. Soon after my arrival the church held its annual synod meetings. No one asked a mere new-comer like me for their opinion, so I sat on a narrow little backless bench for five days without saying a word — some of my friends say this is proof that the day of miracles is not over! But this

condition prevented any possibility of my forcing my opinion onto other people.

4. The church laid it down that they would not allow any mission society to have more than one missionary couple serving with them at any one time, so that the mission society would not become too influential or powerful in the life of the church.

We were in fact entirely under the leadership of the church to do what they wanted. And the renewal of our visas each year depended on them continuing their sponsorship of us. Of course it was not always easy living and working in this way, but it forced us to be servants rather than 'experts' — a better pattern for the foreign missionary. And when doors were opened to us we knew they really wanted us. This way of working led to excellent relationships; money, power and expertise often sour relationships.

Jesus said that it is more blessed to give than to receive. Certainly our local believers thoroughly enjoyed giving to us as they observed our needs. They loved to show Elizabeth how to cook the local vegetables and other foods. I needed their help as I struggled to open a coconut and remove its fibre. Paraffin lamps with their recalcitrant wicks defeated us again and again. When we were ill, local ladies took over in the home and cared for us. Christians lavished gifts of rice, eggs, vegetables and fruit on us with the exclamation, 'You have come to bring us spiritual food; you must allow us to give you material goods.'

The fact that none of us like to be always at the receiving end reminded me of Britain after the second

World War. Our American friends were so amazingly generous to us all in post-war Europe, donating so much food and money to us in our poverty. But British pride hated having to receive such charity and our city walls sprouted graffiti saying 'Yanks, go home!' As foreign workers we often need to be reminded of this.

Accepted immediately

As has already been mentioned, many Indonesian churches feared missionary domination after their experiences in the colonial period. They some times therefore tested their missionaries' humility and servant spirit by leaving them for almost a year doing nothing of significance. If the expatriate workers passed that test, the doors opened wide for future ministry. If they failed and insisted on fulfilling what they felt was their calling and their gifts, then their future ministry was doomed to frustration through the church's quiet non-involvement in the missionary's projects.

On my first Sunday in Indonesia I was welcomed to the large Karo Batak church in the big city of Medan. After speeches of welcome I was asked to stand at the door and shake hands with all the members as they trooped out. To my surprise the leading elder shook hands in a way which I thought was only for Muslims — the left hand under the right forearm and then the right hand rises to the forehead. I did not have time to pray or ask for advice on how I should shake hands, so I immediately responded by shaking hands in his way. But then I wondered what to do with all the thousand or so Christians who followed him out of the church, shaking hands with me in various different ways. I decided that it might be best for me to follow the example of the elder and use his method of shaking hands. This I did with all the church members whether men or women, younger or older, wealthy or poor.

I later discovered that this Muslim-style handshake was used in that particular culture only when shaking hands with someone reckoned to be your superior. The elder was reacting to me as if colonialism still prevailed. Although I was ignorantly unaware of what I was doing, I was saying with my handshake, 'No, my brother, colonialism is finished. I am your servant.' I then repeated this message to every single church member by giving them all the Muslim-style handshake.

Because I made this public statement of humility, taking a position below all Indonesian Christians, I was immediately accepted and doors were opened for wide ministry. God is good and overrules our ignorance!

Another interesting thing happened in my early days in Indonesia which also played a part in making me immediately acceptable locally. At the church synod they celebrated its conclusion with a great feast. A whole pig was roasted and everyone was looking forward with eager anticipation to this meal together. Sadly they added so much red pepper that even local Christians could not eat it. But I was the proud missionary who boasted that I always eat whatever is put before me, so I did battle with the pepper. The pepper

won! I soon had perspiration pouring from my forehead; my eyes and nose ran uncontrollably. My face
turned a vicious red. I tried to put more banana and
rice with the pork to soften the effects, but all to no
avail. After a while people began to notice my predica-
ment and their smiles turned into infectious laughter.
The only possible response was to laugh with them.

Many commented that they never expected a European to be willing to laugh at himself. In such a
situation no one could look on me as a proud imperi-
alist! And so God prepared the way for wide ministry.

Fruitful ministry

We soon discovered that in a mass movement situation
the needs were twofold — firstly Bible teaching and
training, then helping local believers to reap the abundant harvest.

Happily I was not ordained and so could not be
ensnared in the round of baptisms, communion services and weddings. Our church had only six ordained
ministers for some seventy five congregations and
they ran from church to church administering the
sacraments. In fact I have sometimes said that they
became like sacramental sausage machines! Meanwhile multitudes wanted to become Christians, so the
church had laid down a rule that no one could be
baptized unless there were at least twenty-five new
believers in the group. We could not afford the time
for a minister to hold a baptismal service for a mere
handful of people.

The danger constantly threatened that the thousands of new Christians would remain untaught.

With the paucity of ordained ministers and their being trapped in the sacramental round, the main work of preaching, teaching, pastoring and evangelizing lay in the hands of untrained laity. Since coming back to England we have observed how British clergy often seem not to have learned to delegate adequately.

In Kabanjahe where we were living, six home groups studied the Bible each week. Several womens' home groups followed the same pattern of consecutive Bible study, each week moving on to the next passage through the New Testament. Both Elizabeth and I regularly attended several of these in order to help teach the Bible and we were thrilled to see how very open people were. We often remarked that the Karo Batak church was like a well-laid wood fire which just needed a match to create a blaze. When we added an emphasis on personal faith to the biblical truths they already believed, they burst into excited life-changing revival.

Elizabeth was asked to train a group of young adults in Sunday School teaching. As a result they started such revolutionary ideas as dividing the Sunday School into classes, singing with the children, using visual aids and having an aim in their teaching. Boredom gave way to vital life and hundreds of children were added to the church. Later Elizabeth's teaching was passed on to other congregations through the vision of those she had trained and the fire spread.

A handful of about thirty teenagers were scattered around the huge church which seated a thousand and lacked good lighting. This inauspicious start to our Monday youth meeting depressed us, but one after another they came to life and began to invite their friends. Numbers grew. We translated some more modern songs to replace the traditional hymns which were always sung at a snail's pace and bored the youngsters. These new songs caught on and youngsters could be heard singing them all over the town. Through this youth meeting each week many lives were changed by the Holy Spirit and the Word of God. It became the source of gossip in the coffee shops and in the homes: 'What is happening in the church? Our young folk have become such lovely people.' Gangsters, nominal Christians, all sorts came to Christ and found new life. Soon they joined me in hospital evangelism and learned on the job how to witness, give a testimony, teach the Scriptures and preach. Some then went back to their own home villages and planted new churches there.

Both Elizabeth and I taught the Christian faith to hundreds of students in secondary schools and colleges in the town. Islam, Roman Catholicism, and Protestant Christianity were recognized religions in Indonesia and it was expected that they should be taught in the schools. At the start of each academic year the pupils chose what religious teaching they would follow that year. The religious teachers lined up, gave a little speech to attract the young people to join their class and then they all joined the crowd in front of us.

I remember one occasion when the Catholic teacher encouraged people towards his line by promising that all would get good marks in their exams! I wondered what to say in response to that. Finally I declared: 'I would encourage all who are lazy or who cheat to join the other lines; but anyone who is honest and works well will get good marks in my class.' Most of the young people joined my class!

We would not only have eighty or so youngsters crammed into each class, but often considerable crowds gathered outside the open door and windows to hear our teaching. Many became Christians; others grew in their faith; some heard God's call to full-time ministry in the church.

Each Sunday we were invited to spend the day in a village church somewhere. Usually this involved a tedious bus trip and an hour or two on foot each way. We would lead their service and preach, have lunch in someone's home and then teach and answer questions for some three hours before wending our weary way home.

About once a month I visited our local leprosarium which was just an hour or two away by bus. Beautiful houses in the local style nestled at the foot of one of the great volcanos. Masses of poinsettia and other sub-tropical flowers added to the outward beauty. But Laosimomo had no drugs at all to help the patients and no one was qualified to advise them on how to live sensibly with their disease. They just rotted there until they eventually died.

I particularly remember one old man with no hands, crippled feet, blind, with no nose left, who lapped his food from the plate like a dog. But he loved the Lord.

'I always thank God that he allowed me to have leprosy,' he told me once. 'If I had not had leprosy and come here, I might never have become a Christian.' He then waved the stumps of his hands before my eyes and added 'I've been here for forty-five years now and soon I shall be with the Lord in heaven.'

Sometimes when I have felt sorry for myself when I have a cold or some minor problem, I remind myself of this man's radiant joy and spirit of thankfulness to God.

With so many churches longing for teaching it was impossible to satisfy them all. By going each Sunday to a different church I was able to reach out to some, but many were asking for more than that. What mission strategy should be followed in such a situation?

I decided to concentrate on those congregations which were most open and responsive, to bring them to dynamic faith which would then spread to the other less lively congregations. Some churches I visited weekly to give them a day's teaching and then go out with them in the evenings to plant a church together. I wanted my teaching to be inseparably linked to evangelism and church planting. Other churches I visited fortnightly or monthly or just very occasionally for a day's teaching plus church planting.

In our own town of Kabanjahe some of the elders and deacons caught the vision for planting churches, but they felt quite inadequate for the job. They asked me to train them in how to do it and we met each week for this class. Happily after a while the class disbanded because they were all so busy in the actual work that they had no time for classes about it.

Village evangelism

As we have already seen in the Introduction to this book, church planting into the surrounding villages became an important part of our ministry. As with every aspect of our work, it had to be firmly under the direction of our local leaders — it must not be 'our work'.

In the post-colonial situation, after centuries of Dutch domination, the church faced the danger of feeling inadequate and unable to take the lead in evangelism.

'If you do it, we will gladly come with you', people sometimes said to us.

As a result we avoided using any material possessions which they did not also have access to: film strips, flannelgraph etc. In this way we could always say, 'Anything we can do, you can do better because you know your people and your language better than we do.'

Likewise when village evangelism developed, we made a point of not going every week with the church planting team. It had to be clear that they were the leaders and we were just assisting them.

This also made it easier for other churches to emulate the example of the church in Kabanjahe, our market town. Because the church planting teams were led by local Karo Batak Christians, other churches in the area felt able to start planting churches too. So a whole new movement developed which really took off even more after we had left.

Revived missionary?

Since returning to Britain we have observed people's attitudes towards us. If we tell them about our work in Indonesia with the enormous growth of the church, multitudes of radically changed lives and an amazingly fruitful ministry, then people admire us as spiritually vital Christians with a clear experience of the Holy Spirit. They will then listen to what we say with open ears. If on the other hand we talk about our work as pioneer missionaries among Muslims with no churches planted and nobody converted, then reactions are quite different! We are then considered to be boringly traditional missionaries who know nothing of the power of the Holy Spirit in ministry!

So did we experience revival on the plane between South Thailand and Indonesia? The very question borders on the ridiculous. No! We were no better as missionaries in Indonesia than we were in Thailand — or, to put it the other way round, we were no worse as missionaries in Thailand than we were in Indonesia. In his sovereign grace God has his time for each people and nation; he is the Lord of history. It is God alone who opens doors for the gospel and who keeps doors relatively shut. Our task is to pray that God would open a door for his word (Col. 4:3), to enter through those doors he does open and to preach the gospel relevantly and powerfully wherever God places us.

While in South Thailand I had attended a conference for all our workers there. The speaker talked about God adding daily to his church by the power of the Holy Spirit. He then challenged us to repent, be reconciled to each other, be filled with the Spirit. He promised us that if we were filled with the Spirit, then God would bring growth to his church. Many of the OMF workers experienced emotional scenes of repentance and being filled with the Spirit. Two of us however watched with some scepticism — was this a genuine work of the Spirit or just tired missionaries longing for fruitfulness?

It was reported widely that revival had hit the OMF in South Thailand. Sadly it did not prove true. Our workers returned to their various towns and their conference experience made no difference at all to their work among Muslims and Buddhists. People still did not come to faith in Christ. Most of those who had experienced the so-called revival returned disillusioned to their home countries within a year or two.

Group movements

I had never before seen whole groups turning to Christ together. In South Thailand therefore I missed the opportunities which presented themselves for such movements.

Before I arrived in North Sumatra a whole battalion of the Indonesian army had turned to Christ. I was told that the officers had called a parade together where the claims of the Christian faith had been discussed with the opportunity for any man to support or oppose these claims. Finally it had been agreed that they should become Christians, the church gave baptismal preparation classes to the whole battalion, and then they were, baptized en bloc. The baptismal preparation included repentance for wrong relationships and sinful behaviour in the barrack room. Now the Holy Spirit would bring new life and other units of the army could watch to see what difference the Christian faith makes in the daily life and work of an army battalion.

During my time in Indonesia I had the joy of leading a hospital ward to faith in Christ. I found it challenging to see how the Indonesian Christians witnessed to groups of people and encouraged them to become believers together.

After my time in Indonesia, but as a result of our teaching, a secondary school of some five hundred teenagers turned to Christ. The school was located in an area where communism had a strong influence and I had given teaching to the church leaders there which showed up the dangers of communism. This had caused enormous problems with threats of my being accused of high treason because the communist party was an officially recognized political party in the independent state of Indonesia. The communists held open-air meetings and visited from house to house to denounce me. But when in 1965 the communists attempted a coup d'etat and it failed, everyone could see for themselves the threat communism posed and a fierce anger against communists erupted throughout the land. Then people remembered that in my teaching I had warned them and they saw that it was Christians who had stood out against communism. This led to the whole school wanting to follow the Christian faith because it represented the truth.

More recently when teaching about group movements to Christ, I have realized that we also often make such communal decisions. As a faculty at All Nations we discuss an issue and then make a decision together. It has sometimes happened that I have not been convinced that the decision made has been right. Then I have to ask myself whether it is such a matter of principle that my only option is to resign — happily I have never found myself in that position! Otherwise I can only submit to the majority, loyally support the implementation of the decision and see how it works out. Sometimes after a while I see that the majority were right and I am converted to their opinion. Sometimes I observe that other staff members are also beginning to question the wisdom of the decision we took. Then perhaps one can ask that the issue be discussed again.

A similar process unfolds with group conversions to Christ. The majority really believe in the Lord and are convinced of the truth of the gospel. A small minority may have their doubts, but will loyally support the Christian faith because they are part of the group. Of course if someone strongly opposes Christ, then they will have to disassociate themselves from the group's decision. After a year or so the doubters will observe the outworkings of the new faith in their group. Hopefully they will then see the beautiful fruit of the Holy Spirit evidenced in their friends' lives and will themselves therefore really come to faith. Meanwhile they are at least within the covenant people, receiving teaching, feeling the reality of worship and partaking in the loving fellowship of Christians.

Why so open?

When God is at work, a variety of different influences join together to further his purposes. It is not easy to give neat answers to the question of why people in North Sumatra showed such openness to the Christian faith. Perhaps four ingredients should be noted here.

a) The Christians' confidence

'Are you a Christian yet?' 'No, I'm still a Muslim.'

So ran the common greetings when strangers met on a bus or in a coffee shop. Christians assumed that the natural progress lay in becoming a Christian. But when a Muslim greeted someone, it was subtly different:

'Are you a Muslim?' 'No, I'm a Christian.'

In more recent years the Muslim population of our area of North Sumatra has become much more self-confident with a new assurance of the superiority of Islam. But in our day it was the Christians who unconsciously assumed that anyone with common sense would want to become a Christian.

This contrasts markedly with many Christians in Britain where we lost the intellectual battles a century or so ago and Christianity ceased to be the obvious option for intelligent, go-ahead people with a high moral sense. As a result many Christians are defensive about their faith, frightened to enter into debate with non-Christians and unsure that Christ really does have sufficient answers to the problems and weaknesses of our society. But the charismatic renewal is giving people greater confidence in witness. Some may accuse such churches of triumphalism, but defeatist churches and unsure Christians need to regain assurance that life and salvation in Christ can transform both individuals and whole societies.

b) *Marriage*

In Muslim and tribal religious circles the heartbreak of divorce spreads pain and uncertainty through many families. In our day the Christian church stood firmly opposed to divorce and thus gave a much greater security to marriage. 'I wish I were a Christian and could have a Christian marriage', some people would say to us. And we would point out how marriage depends on love, willingness to confess wrongs and to forgive, mutual honouring and serving — indeed on the presence of Christ as well as Christian principles.

We have been sad to see how the British churches struggle with the breakdown of marriage in our society and have allowed this to infiltrate the church too. Of course we all know the tragedy of marriage relationships which break down and seem irreconcilable. All of us know personally Christians who have come through the tragedy of a broken marriage. None of us wants to show a hard legalistic face which has no empathetic love for our brothers and sisters facing such problems. But still we long for the Christian church in Europe to demonstrate the beauty and security of Christian marriage. We need to do all we can to build such marriages in our churches as well as to pastor lovingly those whose marriages fail.

In North Sumatra Christian marriage attracted

many to Christ. How one wishes this were the case in Europe too!

c) Progress

Things change rapidly in modern Indonesia which has become one of the Pacific Tigers. But in our day the rush into industrial development and high tech modernity had hardly begun.

Indonesian education was pioneered by Dutch missions and therefore Christianity lay at the heart of modern thought. Islamic education consisted largely of rote-learning and was centred on the Arabic Qur'an, which did not prepare people for modern life. Christianity was known as the progressive religion. People with vision and dynamic tended to look to the Christian church as the foundation for progress.

d) An Indonesian religion

As we have seen, Indonesian Christianity is no modern upstart. Its roots lie deep in the history and culture of the nation. Whereas Islam constantly quotes the Qur'an in Arabic, Christians use only the Indonesian language. Although the church buildings, the liturgy, hymns and clerical gowns stem from Holland, they have over the centuries become an integral part of Indonesian culture. No one thinks of them as a foreign imposition.

We have already observed that the greatest stumbling-block to the acceptance of Christ in Asia is that Christianity is seen as a western faith which is alien to Asia. Sadly in more recent years we have seen a host of western missions rushing into Indonesia, building their own empires and setting up their own little foreign denominations and para-church movements. These churches and movements contain the inherent danger of giving the Christian faith a foreign image and thus damaging the witness of indigenous churches.

With the opening up of the former communist countries of Eastern Europe and the Soviet Union the same western insensitivity and proud empire-building may be observed. Too much money, material goods, professional skills and dynamic lead easily to spiritual imperialism, particularly when such Christians receive no adequate mission training.

Chapter 6

Indonesia — More Lessons to Learn

When we think of Indonesia our minds are flooded with a tidal wave of impressions. Never before had we witnessed a mass movement of the proportions seen in North Sumatra in those days. Coming from the relatively stagnant British church we soon realized that we had so much to learn. It was here too that we set up our first home together as a married couple, so Indonesia still lies close to our hearts and fresh in our memories. And what rich experience God gave us in the Karo Batak church — and with so many lovely warm-hearted Christian friends. No wonder two chapters are needed for Indonesia, although our time there was actually quite short. God worked so wonderfully during our two years of ministry there that it seemed like a whole lifetime — in those two years hundreds of lives were radically touched by the Lord, churches were planted, new patterns of evangelism developed and the foundations were laid for the massive growth which came after we left.

Teaching mission

Just south from Kabanjahe lies the homeland of the great Toba Batak people who are virtually one hundred per cent Christian. They are a powerfully gifted people with business acumen rivalling even the Chinese. Sadly their dynamic energy has sometimes boiled over in terribly acrimonious quarrels and splits. How much better if it had been spent in out-going evangelism and mission among other Indonesian races and the wider world overseas.

Our Karo Batak people faced the same danger. They too abound in gifts and dynamic energy. When we worked among them the church still formed only a minority and much evangelism remained to be done, but we could foresee the day when they too would become largely Christian as a people. Would they then follow in the footsteps of their larger neighbours and devote their energies to fierce divisions in the church?

North of us lived the fanatical Aceh people, the first race in Indonesia to receive Islam nearly eight hundred years ago. Between the Aceh and Karo Batak peoples two other races can be found, the Gajo and the Alas. They form a bridge between the strongly Muslim Aceh and the increasingly Christian Karo Bataks. In language and culture they also stand between, so that it is easy for the Karo Bataks to relate to their Alas neighbours. Among the Alas Islam is mixed with traditional tribal religious practices and beliefs, so they are less fanatical than their Aceh cousins. We tried to encourage Karo Batak Christians to begin evangelism and plant churches among the Alas with the further aim of reaching eventually to the Aceh also.

We knew we might hit our heads against a brick wall. Just as the original Jewish apostles did not find it easy to reach out beyond their own people to the Gentiles, so also the Karo Batak Christians seemed often to wear racial blinkers. There was still so much work to be done among their own people! None of us finds it easy to widen our horizons.

But our young people responded warmly when encouraged to lift up their eyes and look at ripe harvest fields around the world. At one stage I decided to give some mission teaching to the hundred or so who attended the Monday youth evening. Alongside the regular biblical teaching I gave them a series of thirty ten-minute snapshots of other countries. Ten different countries were chosen with three short talks about each. In the first talk I introduced the country to them with some basic information about its people, its geography and history. Then followed something about the overall religious scene, for our folk had little idea whether these countries were fundamentally Muslim, Buddhist, Roman Catholic or what. In that second talk they also learned a little about the Protestant churches. Finally they were introduced to one particular church, local Christian family or missionary there so that they could focus their prayers on something or somebody specific.

I remember particularly the reactions when they

learned about a struggling group of five believers in a large North African city. In the mass movement situation of North Sumatra they could hardly imagine such a small group in a huge city. Their hearts melted as they heard of the persecution and the difficulties of being surrounded by a sea of Islam.

'We must send them a gift to encourage them', one of the young leaders announced. 'Next Monday we'll have a tin at the back and we can all put in some money.'

What a business! Their Indonesian rupiahs were changed into American dollars through the OMF's banking system and passed on to a mission working in North Africa. They then gave the money to the little group of local Christians. Our folk also wrote a letter in Indonesian. I translated it into English and the North African worker put it into Arabic. The reply went through the same complicated channels. But the North African Christians were thrilled to know that a large Indonesian church loved them and prayed for them. They were not alone in their faith; they belonged to the worldwide Christian family. And our Christians were challenged by the dedicated suffering of their North African brothers and sisters.

I learned the importance in all situations of teaching Christians about the church worldwide. All of us need reminding that we belong to a great family. We all have a responsibility to pray lovingly for that wider family — and we also have much to learn from Christians elsewhere.

Christian literature

Owing to the extreme inefficiency of the Indonesian postal system in those days our senior missionaries in the city of Medan had not managed to obtain any money for us. We therefore moved to Kabanjahe with nothing but six Indonesian Bibles to sell; even our luggage had not yet arrived!

'People up there don't read, and certainly not Indonesian,' we were told. 'They generally use their own Karo Batak language.'

But when we displayed the Indonesian Bibles, people rushed to buy them. We used the money to go back to the city and buy more Christian literature. We had to live off the profits from these sales and so haggled for good discounts!

Soon the little book table in our home drew people to us like a magnet. Christians were hungry for teaching and devoured every book we could find for them. Often people would ask us if there were any new Christian books in Indonesian as they had read everything I had on my booktable.

With inflation at ten per cent a week throughout our time in Indonesia, we found it very helpful to live off sales of books as we could match the prices to the rate of inflation. We did not depend on getting actual cash through the post — that would lose much of its value during the time the post took to get from the capital city to us.

After a while we found we were selling some twenty-five Bibles or other books each day. On average we had one person a week coming to us with the testimony that they had been converted or experienced some major blessing from the Lord through our books. Children came in hordes to buy small packs of tracts and these were widely scattered in our whole area.

When we took the service and preached on Sundays in the various villages, we always carried a heavy bag of books with us. After the service we would display the literature and the Christians would fall on the books like vultures. Often on the Monday someone from the church would come to our house to buy yet more books.

Soon we found we were making more profit than we needed. Of course we required money to build up our stocks and widen our selection of books. But still quite large sums remained. We decided to give a good book to each of the students we taught in the secondary schools and colleges. Each term therefore we gave out many hundreds of books which complemented our regular teaching of the Bible and bore considerable fruit.

So Indonesia taught us the importance of using Christian literature in our ministry. Since then we have always taken books to sell wherever we go. Still today we put up a book table in each church where we speak and sell thousands of books each year. Often when we visit a church someone will tell us that they have received blessing through a book they bought from us on a previous occasion. God uses Christian books for his glory.

Our sort of church?

When I worked in South Thailand, all the little
churches there practised believers' baptism only, while
in our area of Indonesia all the churches believed in
infant baptism. As a result obvious questions confronted us.

In North Sumatra missionaries of believers' baptism
persuasion had to ask themselves whether they could
in good conscience work in churches practising infant
baptism. If the answer was 'no', they faced two possi-
bilities. Either they could try to found new churches in
direct competition with the already strong national
churches or they would have to say that their theology
closed the door to that part of Indonesia.

As one who believes in the covenantal theology of
infant baptism I rejoiced in the Indonesian situation
and felt at home, but I had to confront the same issue
in South Thailand. Although I was convinced that the
churches there struggled with particular weaknesses
because of their theology and practice concerning baptism, this problem was not in my opinion of central
importance. So I was most happy to work in and with
the policies of that area.

Since those days I have observed how often Christians face this same issue. They move into a village or
a particular area of a city where the local church does
not match their theology or spiritual experience. This
may relate to the question of baptism, forms of worship and church order, the charismatic experience or
some other potentially divisive matter. They then have
to decide whether they can fit into the local church or

whether they feel compelled to commute to a church elsewhere. If they choose the latter response, their local witness will never be very effective.

We noticed in North Sumatra the tragic consequences of working in competition with the national churches. At least once a week I visited our neighbouring town of Brastagi for Bible teaching and training. We had many friends there and reckoned to know the town gossip. However, it was some while before we discovered that an independent evangelical missionary had worked there for some years just before our time in North Sumatra. Although Brastagi, like other Karo Batak areas, was experiencing a mass movement to Christ with multitudes of radically changed lives, this missionary had finally returned to his home country fruitless and discouraged. We asked our Brastagi friends about him.

'He wasn't a Christian', they told us confidently. 'He was a Jehovah's Witness or some sect. So we didn't listen to his teaching, although he seemed quite a nice person.'

I assured them that he was a good evangelical Christian, but they remained adamant. They knew for certain that he was not a Christian.

'He never joined us in worship in the church. He never came to our home groups to study God's word with us. He did not want to have anything to do with the church or God's people.'

The independent missionary had tried to set up new churches of his own background. He had not felt happy with the existing churches which practised infant baptism, used liturgy in their worship, belonged to the ecumenical World Council of Churches, smoked and drank beer — what a catalogue of characteristics! Those who supported him would never have agreed to him working with such churches.

'The Bible is very clear', the Karo Batak Christians continued. 'Anyone who is a believer will love their sisters and brothers, so they will surely want to join with them in fellowship, worship and the reading of Scripture. We should not "forsake the assembling of ourselves together" (Heb. 10:25).'

I had to ask myself who was more biblical, our local Christians or the good evangelical missionary! Had traditional prejudices replaced more important biblical principles?

And what a sad tragedy! A Christian worker of his biblical background and mission experience could have fulfilled such a significant role in the movement of God's Spirit through his people in that area. What a fruitful ministry he could have had! But he was more exclusive than the Holy Spirit who seemed to delight in working in those Reformed churches!

Who is the boss?

'Ganyang Malaysia! Ganyang Inggeris! Spit out the English!' With the formation of the independent state of Malaysia Britain suddenly became the enemy of Indonesia. Vitriolic speeches burst onto the airwaves. Violent demonstrations ran through the streets like a stream of red-hot volcanic lava. The British consulate library in the nearby city of Medan was looted and destroyed. The consul himself stood at the top of his staircase with drawn pistol to hold the crowds at bay while his wife and child hid in a bedroom.

Hearing the constant barrage of anti-British invective, we wondered what we should do. The consul sent us a letter telling us to have our things packed and to be ready for immediate withdrawal. He would send a vehicle to pick us up, but we must be prepared to leave immediately. The car would wait only a few minutes.

Leading local Christians came to our home with words of reassurance.

'You're one of us,' they comforted us lovingly. 'We'll stand with you and won't allow anyone to harm you.'

How glad we were to belong to a strong Indonesian church! In a very personal way we appreciated again the importance of good relationships with local Christians.

But should we submit to the British government representative with all his political authority? Or should we yield ourselves to the authority of our Indonesian church leaders? Or should we somehow try to consult with our mission leaders a thousand miles away in the capital city? And what about our home churches? Did they have the right to play a part in the decision facing us? Or did we personally have to find God's will for ourselves, listening to the advice of others but ultimately making up our own minds? How does God channel his authority to his children?

Clearly our home churches could not possibly appreciate the situation with any intimate understanding. They were too far removed and it was also impossible to consult with them. Likewise we felt that even our mission leaders in Indonesia could not see the particular circumstances and developments in Kabanjahe.

We realized that we had to decide between the British political leaders and our church in Kabanjahe. We lacked confidence in the wisdom of the British consul and wondered how well he actually understood Indonesia and Indonesians. And we felt cocooned in the strength and loving care of our local Christian friends.

Our suitcases remained unpacked.

We felt grateful too that our mission leadership in Jakarta had already shown us that they trusted us fully in all matters. George Steed, the mission director, had told us to keep him in touch with what we did each month, but he encouraged us to make our own decisions without feeling the necessity to consult him. He realized the difficulties of communication between Jakarta and Kabanjahe, so knew that he was not in a position to make decisions for us. His constant appreciation of us and our work gave us a warm feeling; and it was good to know that we were totally free to take holidays when we wanted, to use money as we felt right, to follow whatever strategy of ministry God led us into, and now to stay or to leave in the face of political danger. Since then we have often referred to George Steed's leadership as an ideal model — he encouraged, stimulated and advised us while still treating us with a free hand.

Confront or softly-softly?

When reading the book of Acts a British Christian may
be disturbed by the shockingly direct and even con-
frontational approach of the apostles in their evangelistic preaching. We feel that such approaches border
on the impolite and are therefore unacceptable. But
when we look at mission history we often find that
earlier missionaries sometimes openly attacked local
idolatry or superstition as they declared the uniqueness
of God the creator and Jesus Christ as Lord and
Saviour.

The pioneer missionaries among the Karo Batak had
adopted this way of declaring the truth. Outside one
village a large field was thought to be sacred. If anyone
ventured to walk on it, they would fall seriously ill and
die. The first missionary in that area summoned all the
villagers to witness him walking solemnly across the
field in the name of Jesus Christ.

'Our God stands above all demonic spirits', he
declared. 'Those who trust in him have nothing to fear.'

Trembling with fear the villagers awaited the spirits'
retribution. Would the missionary collapse and die in
the middle of the field? Or would he fall ill that night
at home and die more slowly? What would happen? In
answer to prayer God protected that man from all
demonic attack and nothing at all happened. Many in
that village came to faith in Christ through that daring
challenge which vividly showed that our God stands
above all other spirits. He alone is to be trusted.

But the same missionary later confronted a different
superstition. A strange myth had evolved among the

Karo Batak people concerning a girl who became pregnant outside marriage. She was evicted from her village and then gave birth to three children — a huge snake with eyes the size of a football, a cannon (not ecclesiastical!) and a green princess with hair several miles long. Each morning the green princess combed her hair before the admiring gaze of the village youth. To win the hand of the green princess her suitor had to provide a bride price of one ox a day to feed her brother, the snake. When on one occasion she was snatched away by the prince of the Aceh people to the north, the cannon fired a mighty shot to sink the ship and the snake swam out to rescue the princess. The force of firing the cannon shattered it — and I personally have seen the scattered remnants of the cannon around that village when I have been there to preach.

The missionary heard this tale and laughed at it. It was obviously too ridiculous to be true. He challenged the villagers to unravel the ball of her hair which they kept in the roof of one of their traditional houses.

In front of the whole village the precious symbol of their tradition was produced. All eyes were fixed on it as the elders unwound it. Mile after mile it stretched out without a break. The missionary could find no human explanation. He was baffled and admitted that he could not disprove their story.

When I first went to that village, the cult of the green princess still held the people in its grip. The church struggled, remaining weak and small. The missionary's policy of confrontation had backfired.

One Sunday this village of Seberaya invited me to preach. The usual bus journey and long walk brought me to the green princess' centre. I was shown not only the remnants of the cannon, but also the ball of hair — not the snake! It was believed that anyone who saw the snake would die. I duly led the Sunday service with the church liturgy and then preached about our assurance of salvation. We looked at the marks and proofs of that assurance as shown in 1 John. This little rural church had never heard such teaching on the certainty we have that our death is the gateway to glory in the presence of Christ.

One leading young woman was so excited with this truth that she took her Bible home and read it right through from Genesis to Revelation without stopping. She did not sleep or break for food. She wanted to know for sure whether my teaching was true. When she reached the closing chapters of the Bible and had seen that as a believer in Christ she could be totally confident of eternal life, she was thrilled. She so eagerly wanted to be fully with the Lord in his glory! So she found some cabbage fertilizer which was poisonous and drank it. The poison would take four hours to kill and there was no known antidote. During those four hours she went round the village telling people she would soon be in heaven.

'Three more hours and I shall be with Jesus,' she rejoiced. 'Two more hours and I shall enter heaven.' 'One more hour and I shall be with the Lord I love and who loves me.'

And so she died. People saw the reality of her faith in Christ and the glory of eternal life. As a result hundreds and hundreds turned to the Lord. If eternal life with Christ is so precious and so real, then it is

worth abandoning the green princess and following
Christ.

The question remains. When and how should we
definitely confront false religion? And when should we
just preach the gospel and believe that through the
word of God the Holy Spirit will deliver from false-
hood and change lives? I learned that there is no easy
answer.

God answers prayer

Much water had passed under the bridge of life since
my early days as a committed Christian at Oxford. The
absolute assurance of God working miracles in answer
to prayer had slipped away as I learned to walk by
faith, not by sight. But now in Kabanjahe we desperately needed God's active intervention in very practical
matters.

Living conditions were far from easy. It was not only
that there was no running water or electricity in the
house, but at one stage the whole water system for our
town broke down. After some days the local river a
mile or so out of town became so overcrowded that it
was almost impossible to get water there. It was the
dry season and the sky remained cloudless. Without
adequate water to wash our downstairs room frequently, the fleas hopped in mercilessly from the street
immediately outside.

By this time we had our first child, and a small baby
needs quite a lot of water with nappies to wash.
Eventually we agreed that if God did not bring rain

during the next twenty four hours, Elizabeth and baby Andrew should leave Kabanjahe and move to the city.

There was nothing more we could do except pray — and pray we did! We prayed with all our hearts for rain. And God graciously answered.

The next afternoon we noticed the clouds gathering and the wind began to increase. Then the first heavy drops splashed onto the ground. Soon the heavens opened and it poured. The first minutes of rain washed the roof clean and then we began to gather the water as it rushed down the broken drainpipe outside our house. We filled our water tank behind the house; we filled our buckets; we filled every saucepan, pot and pan. Even the metal containers from our trunks came into service. The water from that downpour sufficed until the town's water-pump was repaired and the town again had water.

The next day crowds came to Kabanjahe for the weekly market. As usual many visited our home.

'Wasn't that rain storm fantastic?' we commented. 'And it's still the dry season! How good of the Lord to give us such rain now!'

'We didn't get any rain', person after person replied. 'But we don't need it so badly in our village.'

Finally we realized that the rain fell only on our town — a mile or so beyond Kabanjahe was the limit of the rain. We praised God; he does answer prayer.

Although we look back on our time in Kabanjahe as a wonderful experience of rich friendships and incredibly fruitful ministry, it was also a period of constant illness.

On one occasion Elizabeth was given penicillin. An

angry spreading rash made her realize that she was allergic to it. Wonderfully the reaction passed without serious consequences. As Elizabeth has described in *God Can Be Trusted*, Andrew nearly died when just a few days old. Without oxygen we would have lost him, and even with it he was within just a few minutes from death. In answer to her heart-cry in prayer, God led Elizabeth to take him to the only hospital in North Sumatra which had oxygen.

I suffered badly from asthma, but we could not get modern sprays or other adequate medicines. One night in desperation the doctor gave me an injection of adrenaline straight into an artery. I felt the rushing of waters through my whole body and then slipped into a deep sense of peace. The doctor thought I had passed away. He and Elizabeth prayed urgently — and after what seemed like an eternity God answered their prayer. I came through with no harmful effects.

Often the asthma made me so weak that Elizabeth had to help me get dressed and walk to the church. She even helped me to climb the steps into the pulpit to preach. Again and again God gave miraculous strength to preach and teach with God-given fruitfulness.

In the midst of one of our annual cholera epidemics we needed a booster injection. Although the local hospital left much to be desired, we had no other choice. The nurse must have hit a nerve with my injection, for I felt a shooting pain and passed out. When I recovered consciousness, my arm was paralyzed and remained immovable for three days. Again we could only pray and trust God for his help. Gradually movement came back to the arm and it returned to normal.

But we had to pray in faith not only for our personal needs. With all the spiritual openness around us we felt our need of God's help.

For example, we saw the strategic importance of one whole area of the Karo Batak church, but no invitations came to minister there. We did not know why. But we prayed that God would open a door to Tigabinanga, the central town of that 'diocese'.

One day the leader of the Tigabinanga church happened to hear me speak. 'I had not realized that you now speak Indonesian properly', he remarked to me. 'You must come and minister in our church too.'

It turned out that he had heard me preaching when I first arrived in Indonesia and my Indonesian still reflected the South Thailand dialect. He had therefore determined not to invite me to minister in his area, for he did not want his churches to receive inadequate teaching from a foreigner without a good command of language. How important it is that missionaries learn the language really well.

But now after months of prayer God opened the door for a fruitful work in the whole area of Tigabinanga. We were also very aware that this 'diocese' bordered on the Muslim areas to the north which we longed for the Karo Batak church to evangelize.

Sometimes of course God answers prayer in ways which we do not expect or want. We cannot force God to work in the exact way we choose. As we have seen, the Japanese missionary writer Kosuke Koyama in his *Waterbuffalo Theology* (SCM 1974) shows how God cannot be compared with some domesticated animal who merely does our bidding.

One Sunday after preaching and teaching in a far-off town I was waiting expectantly for the bus home. A couple of hours slipped cheerfully past in animated conversation with local Christian leaders, but no bus was to be seen. Then someone informed us that the only bus to serve that town had broken down irreparably, so we began to try thumbing a lift from the rare vehicle to pass that way. Nothing stopped — we thumbed some more — still nothing stopped.

Day turned into night. With no street lights to hinder, the multitudes of stars shone brightly. I began to wonder whether I would ever get home. My mind rushed around all the engagements I had for the next day, indeed for the next week. How long would I be stuck in this town? Anxiety yielded slowly to prayer, 'Somehow, Lord, please get me back home tonight.'

A large enclosed lorry saw our desperate signals and screeched to a sudden halt.

'There's no room in the cab', the driver said. 'But you're welcome to go in the back, if you want.'

We looked inside. The lorry was stacked high, almost to the roof, with pigs. Each animal had its own basket and they were then piled one on top of the other. I had no option and climbed up over the pigs to the top. There was not enough space to sit up, but I could recline across the pig-baskets.

We set off along the winding, pot-holed road towards Kabanjahe. The suffering pigs squealed at each bend in the road. And as we hurtled into one huge pot-hole after another, they added further to the filth. As my wife has written in *God Can Be Trusted*, 'the only fact for which he could be thankful was that the law of gravity ensured that the pigs' filth travelled downwards! However, the powers of smell had no such limitations, and in the stuffy atmosphere they steadily increased.'

After several hours we eventually arrived in Kabanjahe and I walked into our house at 3.15 a.m. My Sunday suit now had a good farmyard fragrance — and our shortage of water made it hard to remove the legacy of the pigs from my own body and hair!

But God had answered prayer, even if not in the manner I might have chosen! I was home in time for teaching religious education in a college on the Monday morning plus the rest of that day's ministry.

In Indonesia we relied on the foundational fact that God does answer prayer. We needed his miracles for basic living as well as for our work. Each month we needed two officials' signatures on special forms to allow us to buy paraffin and sugar. We could have managed without sugar, but we cooked on paraffin and used it for our lighting too. Getting those precious signatures could never be taken for granted and we made it a matter of special prayer.

With our literature ministry we often received some forty parcels of books at a time. The post office would not deliver them. They put numbers on each parcel, copied those numbers onto official forms and then we could claim our parcels with the forms — if the numbers tallied! '17642, 17643, 17644 . . . there's a parcel here numbered 17645, but you don't have that number on your form.'

I pointed out that they had put the numbers both on the parcels and on my form — and they knew me so well anyway, so they knew those parcels belonged to me. But the numbers had to tally!

'If we had the signatures both of the head and assistant head of the post office we could tear up the incorrect form. Then we could get permission to write out another form with the right numbers — and if we got two more signatures we could even allow you to have that form and thus claim your parcels.'

But often one of the men whose signature I required was away at a wedding or funeral.

We needed prayer. And God showed us again and again how gracious he is.

Polygamy, women and marriage

'In the Karo Batak culture muscular work is traditionally done by women', I informed my wife when we first arrived in Kabanjahe. 'Which of us should queue early each morning at the end of our road to fetch water?'

Carrying water in buckets is heavy work. Should we stand against local culture in this issue? Where does one draw the line between introducing new cultural values and adjusting to other people's culture? So we discussed together Karo Batak ideas concerning the roles of men and women, and how we should behave.

We agreed that in public we should not touch each other nor look at each other in the face. We decided to walk side by side, but with a good space of perhaps a yard between — local women normally walked well behind their husbands. But we felt it good to introduce the idea that men could help their wives with hard physical work.

At 6 a.m. I duly emerged from our house with two large buckets. Several girls rushed to me, offering to take my buckets and carry the water for me. They assumed that Elizabeth must be ill — and as I had no aunts or nieces at hand to do the work in her place, they generously volunteered to serve us. I assured them that Elizabeth was fine and informed them that in my country men also have muscles!

So the queue for water developed. A line of women was followed by a big gap — and then came me! After a further gap more women followed. And so it continued for some months until one day the church minister who lived next door shyly came out with his buckets. His wife was heavily pregnant and his love for her moved him to spare her this hard work of carrying buckets of water. The women showed their gracious Christian character and allowed him to join me half-way up the queue, so that as men we should not stand alone. From then on whichever of us came out later was allowed to join the other man — so some times we got three bites of the cherry in stead of the usual two, six buckets of water rather than just four. And in a hot climate life becomes easier if one can get more water, so we were grateful.

It did sometimes happen that on becoming Christians men learned to work together with their wives. At the end of our road lived an older Christian who had two wives. One day he walked past our house with his two wives and after the usual greetings announced,

'Now that I'm a Christian, I am learning to work too. And now I am able to do quite a decent stint, although of course I cannot rival my wives! They have worked in the fields all their lives, but I'm learning!'

With the growth of the church more and more men began to share in work with the women. This has influenced family life and relationships, helped the local economy and given men a worthwhile lifestyle. It is some times good that Christianity influences cultural change!

Although this clear division of roles prevailed, there was great freedom for women. In contrast to many Muslim societies they could mix freely with men and they had considerable influence in society. In the church too they played a leading role as elders and deacons — and in many Indonesian churches there had long been women ministers, so this never became an issue.

But the church struggled to combat polygamy. They were happy to baptize new believers who were already polygamous on the condition that the man was baptized together with each of his wives, not just the young beauty close to his heart. But once you were baptized, it became unacceptable to take another wife; and if you did, the church excommunicated you. No polygamist could become a leader in the church as a deacon or elder. In this way they sought to follow the biblical patterns, gradually eliminate polygamy as people become Christians, and witness to the world that the church's ideal is monogamy.

We found ourselves in complete agreement with the church's practice in this matter, although we noticed that occasionally the system could be abused. We knew one or two people who, we suspected, delayed their profession of faith and their baptism until after they had married their second wife. But no church practice is immune to abuse.

Elizabeth's role

Throughout our lives it has been a great privilege to serve together. At each stage we have both felt God's calling to work side by side. We are very different personalities with different gifts and styles of working, so we sense that we complement one another. We have always hoped too that our working together may present a witness to Christian marriage and to the equality of ministry between men and women. I have noticed too that the presence of Elizabeth gives me a more everyday human face, making me a family man rather than 'the speaker'.

Our working together began immediately we moved into Indonesia from our honeymoon. We shared together in many aspects of the work in the Karo Batak church. Of course she had also her own particular ministries. She taught in different schools and colleges from me; she expounded the scriptures in the various womens' Bible discussion groups; she ran a Sunday School teachers' course to train new children's workers; she spoke at large women's rallies.

At first Elizabeth travelled with me along the fiercely bumpy roads in the local bus to the various village churches — and her teaching was so appreciated particularly by other women, but also by the men. Then with pregnancy it became unwise for her to risk the baby's safety in this way and her ministry became more limited. As both of us suffered considerable health problems in Indonesia, this curtailment of ministry caused little frustration at that time; later however, as we shall see, in Malaysia Elizabeth did feel very shut-in and restricted when the children were young. Meanwhile, as she has graphically described in her own life-story, the hazardous saga of baby Andrew's birth and early months fully occupied her time and attention.

'We don't love our children like you seem to', a lady church elder commented to us. We could hardly believe our ears, for they seemed to have such deep caring for their children. But our friend insisted. 'We gain honour, pride and pleasure from our children', she said, 'But we don't love them for *their* sake, only selfishly for *our* sake.' When Andrew cried persistently in the middle of the night, we sometimes questioned ourselves too whether we were motivated by true love or by self-interest!

We realized again and again how people watched our life as a family in our relationships together. At each stage of our life both in Indonesia and later in other countries we have been very aware that we inevitably present a model which others observe and sometimes seek to follow. We have therefore found it deeply challenging that we give a truly biblical and loving pattern both in our relationships together and in our various roles in ministry.

The gospel begins with creation

At Oxford I had been taught that the proclamation of the gospel starts with sin and then goes on to the atoning work of Christ, repentance and faith. In Indonesia my eyes were opened to biblical truth in a new way.

Towering above us at over 8,000 feet two beautiful volcanoes smoked continuously — as did most local men! I have already described in *Don't Just Stand There* (IVP '96) how the people of that area were so impressed by the obvious beauty and power of nature that they believed the volcanoes to be the seat of spirit powers. When a group of us climbed one of these mountains, we passed little shrines with offerings to the spirits by the side of the trail. Bananas, eggs and other food lay before the shrine, while cigarettes perched in forked sticks with smoke lazily curling heavenwards.

On arrival at the top our Christian friends began to shout loudly and hurl stones down into the crater with its pools of sickly light blue water and of bubbling mud. Some stones fell into cracks in the rocks, from which steam spurted out with the bad egg smell of sulphur. The stones got caught up in the fierce jets of steam and were hurled hundreds of feet into the air.

'We're not afraid of nature spirits', our friends shouted confidently. 'We believe in God as creator of everything. He made even these volcanoes with all their power.'

We began to notice how Karo Christians normally started their evangelistic preaching with the fact of

God as the creator of everything. If God is the creator, we are fools to worship spirits of things he has created. God is greater than mere spirits, so we don't need to fear them.

Later I came to realize that in the book of Acts the apostles emphasized the fact of creation in their preaching to Gentiles. So Paul urged the Lycaonians to 'turn from these vain things to a living God who made the heaven and the earth and the sea and all that is in them' (Acts 14:15). Likewise in his Areopagus sermon to the people of Athens he started by proclaiming 'the God who made the world and everything in it' (Acts 17:24). Of course when preaching to Jews the apostles did not need to teach about God as creator — they believed that already. In Acts most of the apostolic sermons were delivered to Jews; only the above mentioned two were given to gentiles.

When I finally returned to Britain I faced the difficulty of presenting an evangelistic message to British gentiles. The story of creation has become so controversial because of the battle over evolution that it is not so easy to follow the biblical pattern and begin an evangelistic message with this foundational truth. Mention of creation can easily lead to our being sidetracked. But with the increase of old paganism and a renewed emphasis on mother earth and nature religion, the absolute greatness of God as the creator of everything gains significant relevance today.

Chapter 7

Malaysia — Chinese, Malay Muslims and my Jewishness

The time came for us to return to Britain for our home assignment. We assumed that we should return again to Indonesia, but it was not to be. The political situation meant that the government refused our application for a return visa. So our mission leaders asked us to fulfil a particular calling in Malaysia.

The earlier missionaries who planted the English-speaking church in Kluang formed it as a Brethren Assembly — their own denominational background. But all the other English-language churches in our state were Presbyterian; and our church met in the Chinese-speaking Presbyterian Church's building; and various of our leaders were the children of the members of that Presbyterian Church.

As good Anglicans ourselves and members of an

inter-denominational mission our task was to convert this little Brethren Assembly into a Presbyterian Church! While having to convince our people that infant baptism could be squared with scripture, we were not required to have them rebaptized as babies!

When our church fitted more easily into the fellowship of the indigenous Chinese churches around, it began to grow.

Our church had started with a few small children coming to the home of a missionary for orange squash and a Bible story. Little tigers become big tigers — and gradually these youngsters grew into teenagers and into adulthood. More children were added at each stage. By the time we came, the church had about fifty baptized young people and a crowd of children, but no mature adults. Our oldest member was twenty-eight years old and she was considered almost fit for a museum! This meant that the church never lacked lively enthusiasm or spiritual vitality, but we were seriously short of mature wisdom and the benefits of long Christian experience. Youth churches need the input of older Christians just as elderly churches would gain from an infusion of youthful dynamic. This was particularly true in a Chinese culture which respected age.

We therefore did everything possible to woo older people to the church, devoting much time and energy to our relationships with them. We started a Sunday service which related culturally more to mature adults, knowing that the teenagers were catered for in other meetings.

In coming to work in Malaysia we had many new

things to learn. Although we had related to Chinese in Singapore before we went to Indonesia, we now discovered how little we knew of their culture and religion. We also had some Hindu and Sikh converts, so we were forced to learn to understand something of their backgrounds too. Visiting the families of the different young people in our church put us into close touch with people from each of these religious backgrounds. We had to think through and learn how to relate the good news of Christ to the various backgrounds.

We soon discovered too that what worked in Indonesia seemed unsuited to our Malaysian situation. As in Indonesia, we longed for a church planting ministry to begin in the unevangelized villages around our town. Again we encouraged the Christians to gain a vision for this and start work. But they were only young people with no standing in a Chinese age-conscious society. After a while we realized therefore that, unlike Indonesia, we needed to take the lead. So we began taking a team out to one village, but soon discovered that Chinese villages in Malaysia are radically different from Karo Batak villages. They are tough nuts to crack and we made little headway.

God was teaching us that you cannot simply transfer fruitful patterns of ministry from one country to another. In Britain this lesson has proved helpful. Of course we can learn from and be inspired by American or Korean churches, but we shall have to fit their patterns to our own situations.

I'm a Jew!

The Lord's gracious love had inspired me to love him
in return; his word in the Bible had become deeply
meaningful in my life; I had seen his Holy Spirit
marvellously at work. And yet the Christian faith had
always hung on me like a beautiful jacket made of top
quality material, but which does not fit across the
shoulders. In my personal insecurity I had blamed my
shoulders, assuming that my sin and weakness somehow alienated me from the glories of Christ as expressed in his church.

Then to my great joy I found myself at home in the
Indonesian church — it fitted me. But it was impossible
in Indonesia to think through the reasons for this. Life
was far too busy for serious reflection in the midst of
such a mass movement to Christ.

But now in Kluang I enjoyed the opportunity to
think and study. Being the pastor of such a small
church did not fill my time. Each week I travelled down
to Singapore to lecture at a Bible College, but still many
hours remained.

I began to look at the Bible and at Christian theology
from a more Jewish perspective. As children my brothers and I knew we stemmed from a Jewish background,
but it meant little to us. Our mother had reacted
against her Jewish background and been baptized as a
Christian in order to relate to English people. Although
as a Christian I had come to love a Jewish Saviour and
was reading the Jewish scriptures, I had little understanding of what it meant to be Jewish. All my education took place in ordinary gentile schools and

university. My theological college was entirely gentile. My friends reflected the gentile environment in which I was brought up.

At last in Kluang my racial background caught up with me. It changed my understanding of the Bible and my approach to Christian theology. Particularly I saw how the universal church has grown out of its roots in the congregation of Israel. Pentecost is by no means the birthday of the church, for the Greek word for 'church' is just the translation of the Hebrew word for 'congregation'. I came to see the early church's danger of becoming a mere sect of Judaism, in which Jewish believers in the messiah and gentile proselytes or God-fearers could find salvation. The New Testament emphasizes that Jesus has come as the Saviour for all peoples, Jews and Gentiles. It is possible to be a gentile and a Christian! It is even possible to be English and Christian — people do not need to become members of the people of Israel and submit to the Jewish Law.

As the years have passed since those days in Malaysia, I feel that my Jewishness has been expressed more and more. More recently it has been a great privilege to teach Jewish studies and to be more involved in the issue of evangelism among Jews. As a vice-president of the Church's Ministry among Jewish people (CMJ) and as an active board member of the very Jewish Jews for Jesus, this aspect of Christian ministry has become a priority in my thinking.

It constantly amazes me how controversial Jewish evangelism seems to be among gentile Christians. Some question whether it is indeed right for Christians to preach Jesus Christ to Jews and whether Jews ought to become Christians. Don't Jews have their own way to God through the covenant with Moses? Clearly the biblical question is rather whether it is right to evangelize gentiles and whether gentiles can be followers of the Jewish messiah.

It has hurt me to witness the intolerance of some who oppose evangelism among Jews. Once or twice such Christians have refused even to drink coffee with me as a Jewish Christian. One cathedral invited me to speak on Christian attitudes to other faiths. When they discovered that I was Jewish, they cancelled the invitation — non-Christian Jews were welcome, but they did not believe that Jews should become Christians. Sadly the present Archbishop of Canterbury has not found it diplomatic to support us as Jewish Christians.

But I am deeply grateful to the Indonesian church and for my more relaxed time in Malaysia which helped me to begin the process of entering into my Jewish heritage as a Christian.

Story-telling

'If we really want to communicate effectively to Muslims, we shall have to learn to teach through telling stories.'

These words from Gordon Gray, a brilliant Canadian doctor at Saiburi in South Thailand, struck a chord with me. I shall never forget that evening as we wandered around the beautiful little fishing port of Saiburi in the sultry cool of a moon-lit tropical evening.

I began to experiment right away with the fascinating Jungle Doctor animal stories of Paul White. His stories came from East Africa, but they could easily be adapted to a Malay Muslim audience. I noticed how large crowds of Malays would listen with excitement to these stories. And the moral and spiritual lessons of the stories would never be forgotten.

But then in Indonesia the art of story-telling went into cold storage. People were so open and spiritually hungry that it seemed unnecessary to wrap the gospel in stories.

In Malaysia however I faced a new situation. Having openly distributed large quantities of Malay Christian literature and preached the gospel without any dissimulation to Muslims, I received a letter from the local Sultan. It accused me of disturbing the peace by such preaching which was evidently illegal. Sadly Malaysia lacks full religious freedom. Christians are not permitted to witness to Muslims and Muslims are strictly forbidden to convert to another faith. So I was summoned to a meeting with his representative and the chiefs of police — a gracious invitation it was wise to accept! In consequence of that meeting I had to promise not to take the initiative in preaching about Jesus Christ to Muslims.

But as a Christian I am commanded by God himself to witness to all people of whatever racial or religious background. So what should I do? It was in that context that I remembered Gordon Gray's words and began again to tell stories. As I have described in *Islam and Christian Witness* (O.M. '82), I seem quite incapable of thinking up new stories of my own. But I can take other people's stories and adapt them to a new audience with new applications. So I took over various of Jesus' parables, gave them a Muslim cultural dress and a spiritual application which related to Malay Muslims. In this way I remained true to my promise, but it opened the door for people to ask questions about religion. If they took the initiative, I could answer.

After a while I gained a reputation among Malays as a story-teller. I have since realized what a high position in the entertainment world such a person holds in Muslim societies. In North African and Middle Eastern market squares crowds gather round the story tellers who are highly esteemed.

In more recent years I have been encouraged by various Christian workers among Muslims who have told me that they have successfully used story-telling forms of Christian witness. It is always heart-warming when your students put your teaching into practice! At All Nations Christian College I have taught a course on story-telling for some years.

Over-night conferences

Ours was a haunted house! On the path outside, a strangely misshapen tree was known as the place where someone had died of a heart-attack. A few houses further on lived a witch-like old lady whose vivid red finger nails curved several inches long like a vulture's talons.

No wonder our house could be rented quite cheaply! Having cleansed it from all demonic influence, we could enjoy it. With five bedrooms downstairs and a huge open space upstairs this old wooden house became an ideal centre.

Every month we invited thirty or forty youngsters to come for a day and a night there. Together we enjoyed several sessions of worship and teaching plus the important activity of eating our meals as a fellowship. In the Bible eating and drinking together has vital significance and even in Britain we notice the importance of this in the life of the church.

Crammed into the bedrooms and the upstairs 'dormitory' at night our teenagers opened up more intimately with each other. The older Christians took the opportunity to counsel and encourage the younger Christians as well as often leading the unconverted to faith in Christ. In the mornings they read the Bible and prayed in groups, thus showing newer Christians how to study the scriptures for themselves and how to enjoy times of prayer.

Away from the pressures of non-Christian homes God revealed himself in new ways to many. These regular mini-conferences became the focus of Christian life and growth.

It's foreign!

The opportunity of further study overseas excited her whole family. After a long sea journey Eng Lin was welcomed into a local home. Before the evening meal she was asked if she wanted to use the bathroom and, as is customary in Malaysia, she duly went upstairs to take a bath before dinner. As she would in her own home, she filled the bath full of water, stood on the floor outside and poured large quantities of water over herself. Soon the water began to flow all over the floor, under the door and down the stairs! Her hosts knocked desperately at the door to ask what on earth she was doing.

Adjusting to British life was not always easy! But this Christian home became a loving haven for her. They invited her to come to church with them and she politely agreed. With her acute mind she quickly grasped the truth of the Christian message and she was attracted by the lives of the English Christians she now met.

But she was Chinese. She didn't want to follow a foreign religion. She was deeply conscious of the fact that Chinese civilization and religion stretch right back into antiquity, whereas Christianity is relatively modern. So she continued politely to go to church, but commitment to Christ was not in her mind.

On returning to Malaysia she began to teach in a large secondary school in her home town of Kluang. Another Chinese teacher invited her to accompany her to the church.

'But you're Chinese like me! You can't be a Christian, can you?' she queried. She soon discovered that the church was entirely Asian with nothing but Chinese and Indian members. In a truly Malaysian context she was able to open her heart to the glory of Jesus Christ and become a Christian.

Eng Lin was the most senior Christian in our church and we felt very privileged to share her friendship, wisdom and spiritual insight.

One day we overheard her talking with another Christian teacher, who came from a godly Christian home. What a contrast with Eng Lin's family! Her father had five wives who spent their days and nights gambling at mahjong and consulting Taoist mediums in spirit seances.

'In 1 Cor.8 Paul says that idols have no real existence, so I have no compunction about eating food offered to ancestral spirits', Eng Lin's friend affirmed. 'After all, the chicken is the same after being offered as it was before — a chicken is a chicken is a chicken!'

But Eng Lin counter-attacked, 'Paul also declares that "what pagans sacrifice they offer to demons" (1 Cor.10:20) and he does not want people to be partners with demons. He even says that "you cannot drink the cup of the Lord and the cup of demons." '

Coming from such different backgrounds our two friends saw the biblical teaching from different perspectives. When Eng Lin became a Christian, she felt it necessary to make a clear stand in her very non-Christian home. She refused to eat anything which had been placed on the spirit shelf as an offering to the ancestors. All the meat, vegetables and fruit were put on the spirit shelf in front of her dead father's photo, so for the first six months of her Christian life she ate nothing but rice and tomato ketchup. Finally her mothers relented and cooked some food separately.

Coming into the heart of a Chinese society, we had to think through questions which had not come our way before. Again and again in conferences we heard Christians struggling with the very practical issues of food offered to spirits, what to do in a Buddhist funeral, should you serve tea on your knees to your mother-in-law etc. We began to discover the spiritual power which bound people to the Chinese temples to which they had been dedicated. We learned about the different forms of charms which held sway in their lives. Those who came from more Confucianist backgrounds responded to solid ethical teaching with an application for our lives together in society; they were less interested in dealing with the spirit world or with doctrinal questions. Those from more Buddhist or Taoist homes, on the other hand, often reacted against the spiritually emotional religious life of those faiths; they wanted objective truth, not existential emotion. We had much to learn!

On the other hand, I found that Chinese culture has much in common with our Jewish way of thinking. Family life and social attitudes are similar. Both overseas Chinese and Jews have lived as threatened minorities and have developed closely related feelings of insecurity — and have reacted to that in the same ways. Both esteem learning and education highly. Both have become skilled and industrious business people. It is sometimes said that the Chinese are the Jews of the east — I have often felt that I am a Chinese of the west!

Death and the after-life

Two tragic deaths rocked our church. A young teenager fell through a garage roof, hitting his head on the cement below. Another lad died in a motorcycle accident. Large crowds came to both funerals and the uncertainty of life resounded in everybody's thoughts. What the Puritans called 'seriousness' overcame the easy-going youthfulness of our congregation and we all appreciated afresh the wonderful reality of our salvation through the cross and resurrection of Jesus Christ.

In traditional Chinese contexts the Damocles sword of death and judgement always hangs threateningly over their heads. In Taoist funerals lurid pictures of the fearsome tortures of hell adorn the home of the deceased, so that every child grows up in fear of the agonies which may await them.

Because of such vivid pictures many traditional Chinese continue through life with a burning desire to escape the judgement. In my earlier Christian life in Britain I had reacted against hell-fire preaching, putting little emphasis on salvation from judgement and hell — indeed hell rarely got a mention. But now in Kluang I wanted the gospel to be what it is, namely good news. It had to scratch where people really itch. So I was forced to question my own background as to whether it put blinkers on me. Was I missing one whole dimension of biblical truth? Would I now export to Malaysia the prejudices which came from my British background?

One young leader in our church had become a Christian in order to gain salvation from hell. My predecessor in Kluang had strongly preached that nobody could lose their salvation, stressing that once we are safe in the Father's hands nobody can snatch us away (Jn. 10:28–29). As a result our young friend felt free to abandon his Christian faith, believing that he would still be immune from judgement.

'I'm saved from hell; now I can do what I like', he boldly declared not only to us, but also to all his non-Christians friends. Although he had been one of our leaders, he now no longer followed Christ and settled into a life of rank materialism.

Referring to the so-called 'warning passages' in Hebrews 4, 6 and 10, I urged him to repent and turn back to Christ in whole-hearted discipleship. I declared to him the word of the Lord that 'if we sin deliberately after receiving the knowledge of the truth, there no longer remains a sacrifice for sins, but a fearful prospect of judgement' (Heb.10:26–27)

At the time he did not respond, but later the Holy Spirit used these words to bring him back to the Lord and to his service.

Teaching worldwide mission

As in Indonesia, so too in Kluang we wanted to widen the horizons of the church. We shared this desire with the other leaders and suggested a missionary weekend once a year. They were indignant. Why only once a year? In their enthusiasm they wanted it each quarter. And why only a weekend? They insisted that all the teaching for a whole week should concentrate on worldwide mission. And all the offerings in every meeting must be dedicated to missionary work outside Malaysia.

During our mission weeks every Christian was given a small envelope into which they could put their offerings. They were encouraged to write on the envelope where they wanted their gift to be sent. We noticed with joy that the offerings during a mission week were usually about ten times as much as those on ordinary weeks.

We scattered mission prayer letters and magazines around the congregation, encouraging people to concentrate their prayers on one area of need but at the same time to gain a wide picture of God's work worldwide.

There was just one fly in the ointment. They began to read about work in Asia, including their own Malaysia. One magazine quoted a missionary's letter, asking prayer for someone they all knew — this person was falling into sin and backsliding. The magazine gave more details of the sin she was involved in! Scandal! We need to be sensitive about what we put into print, and aware of who might read it.

At that time our mission had just begun to open its doors to Asians to become missionaries and serve with OMF. With hindsight it seems incredible now that missionary societies were so slow to encourage overseas mission from the churches we planted. I had faced this problem when, as a new missionary in Singapore, I had taught a young adults' Bible class. One of the leading young women felt called to go overseas as a missionary, but back in 1960 there was no missionary society locally which would accept a Chinese applicant. And her local church was not strong enough to support her, as they were largely young people without much money.

But now the OMF began to teach about mission and to hold missionary conferences. I remember the first such conference held in Singapore and the tremendous enthusiasm which local Christians displayed. We were all particularly challenged by a Tanzanian Christian who was passing through Singapore and spoke to us.

'I never before appreciated that there were Chinese Christians', he observed, 'The only Chinese to come to work in Tanzania are communists. Why have no Christians come?'

We thank God that the churches of Singapore and Malaysia are now beginning to shoulder their missionary responsibilities.

Gurkhas and courage

In Kluang a large Gurkha regiment was stationed — and what soldiers they were! They marched smartly as if on parade even when they were going to the bathroom! During the confrontation between Indonesia and Malaysia, it was the Gurkhas who inspired terror among the Indonesian soldiers. British troops they could handle, but the dedicated ferocity of the Gurkhas overwhelmed even the bravest.

Every week a handful of Christian Gurkhas came to our home for fellowship and teaching; and on Sundays they attended our church.

I well remember the embarrassment of their first visit to our house. As was customary, Elizabeth served the guests orange squash and I invited them to drink. My glass was already halfway to my mouth when their leader firmly observed, 'Well, *we* shall pray!' He then led in prayer at considerable length while my glass hovered uncertainly between table and mouth! The Gurkha Christians believe that all things come from the hand of God and therefore it is right to thank him even for a glass of squash.

At one stage only one Christian remained in the Kluang Gurkha camp, but then he led some six others to faith in Christ. The commanding officer heard that soldiers were being converted from their traditional Hinduism. So he summoned the whole regiment onto the parade ground, gave them a stern lecture on the impropriety of Gurkhas becoming Christians and warned of dire consequences for anyone who had the temerity to do such a thing. He then commanded that anyone who was thinking of being a Christian should take one step forward from their ranks.

The whole regiment waited with bated breath. Silence hovered over the parade ground. Then one man smartly marched one step forward, his boots cracking against the asphalt as he clicked to a halt. No one else moved.

The officer went to him and tore him off a strip. When he drew to a close the soldier quietly said, 'Sir, I think perhaps you don't know much about Christianity. If you require to know further, I shall be glad to help.' That evening the officer made his way to the soldier's barracks and agreed that his words had been true. He didn't know much about the Christian faith. The Christian soldier quietly shared with him what Jesus Christ means to a believer.

When relating to the Gurkhas, I often reflected on Paul's constant emphasis on 'boldness' and joined my prayers to his that God would enable me too to proclaim Christ boldly. Since then I have felt it right to add the word 'wisdom'. In our lives and witness as Christians we need the combination of boldness and wisdom; one without the other leads to disaster or ineffectiveness.

Days off

In Indonesia it had proved impossible to take days off. If we stayed at home, visitors thronged the house. If we went out, people could not understand why we were not actually going somewhere — the idea of picnics or just going out to enjoy the beauty had not yet dawned. If we went to the one smarter hotel in our area, most of the waiters belonged to our church and peaceful relaxation was impossible.

So we stored up our sabbaths and from time to time took a whole week away where we knew no one. The beautiful Lake Toba beckoned us with its wild poinsettia and splendid swimming.

Now in Kluang the army allowed us to use their swimming pool. How we enjoyed our weekly day off with the warm pool, lounge chairs and the shade of tropical trees! The children flourished in the shallow pool and close by was an army helicopter station. Andrew and Margaret were fascinated by these great birds constantly taking off and landing. This kept them happily occupied.

We came to appreciate why the Lord had ordered us all to have a weekly sabbath, a day of stopping. We have since observed how many Christian workers smile at this divine ordinance — and in middle age they pay the consequences, gathering up all their accumulated sabbaths and taking them all at once in a hospital or enjoying a breakdown!

A young mother

While in Kluang we had two small children and they were a full-time job. Although the burden fell primarily on Elizabeth's shoulders, we agreed that she needed a break from domestic duties. Once a week I took charge of the children while she led a Bible class and thus gained close contact with certain local Christians. She then had people she knew well and could visit with the children, although it was not easy to push them through the tropical heat in their pushchair.

Inevitably at that stage of family life Elizabeth was tempted to allow her mind to drift along in neutral, concentrating on the daily necessities of small children, nappies, food and sleep. It became important for me to share fully what was going on in the church, to encourage her to continue some serious reading and to talk and pray about wider issues.

But Elizabeth remembers our couple of years in Malaysia as a time of some frustration and loneliness. We have come to appreciate how much parents of young children need encouragement and loving support. They need also to know that time spent in mundane domestic life with small children lays the foundation for good parent-child relations right through life. As those years pass, the children develop and time for other ministries increases.

But for that short period of life the children did require quite careful oversight. For example, our house often had centipedes lurking in dark corners. The walls did not come right down to the floor, allowing some movement of air to keep the house cool. Centipedes loved the dark gaps between the floor and the walls — and Andrew's toy cars seemed also to make a bee-line there! These dusty and dangerous corners also seemed to attract Margaret's fingers. We tried to watch for centipedes and kill them, but inevitably we missed a few. Their sting is so painful that it can kill a small child through shock.

We are grateful to God for his protection of our children — and I am grateful to Elizabeth for her part in God's care for them.

OMF Conferences

Like most missionary societies OMF held workers' conferences each year. What a delight it was to have those days of unrushed fellowship with our fellow missionaries from different parts of Malaysia! One year we all went to Port Dickson to a conference centre right by the sea. Golden orioles flitted through the branches of the flame trees and kingfishers flashed their vivid fluorescent blue along the beach. In many ways that week was idyllic. It was good too to share the scriptures together and to have time to pray for each other in some detail.

The Sunday proved to be the one hazard. In the burning heat of a tropical day the clear blue sea beckoned invitingly beyond the sandy beach. Our two toddlers longed to paddle and play in the shallow waters, but in those days we had one or two senior missionaries whose sabbatarian principles allowed walking but not swimming on a Sunday. Frankly it was much harder 'work' going for a walk in the heat with two small children than to allow them to play in the water. But we knew it would offend these fellow-workers badly if we all changed into swimming costumes — and our unity and fellowship was more important.

We are glad that today in Europe such legalistic attitudes have almost entirely vanished in our current desire for freedom. Perhaps we now run the danger of swinging the pendulum too far in the opposite direction — we are so free from petty rules that we can become careless about obedience in holiness.

The following year I was asked to give the main talks at an OMF conference and wondered what sort of topic would be helpful to our workers. I felt it right to give three addresses on the persons of the Trinity, the Father, the Son and the Holy Spirit. Together we were impressed by the centrality of the doctrine of the Trinity in every aspect of our Christian faith — all the rest depends for its validity on the fact of the Trinity. And without a true emphasis on each person of the Trinity our faith will become unbalanced.

In contrast to the non-trinitarian Jewish and Muslim monotheism, in the Trinity the three persons relate in love and humility together. The Spirit points away from himself to glorify Jesus Christ, so those of us who are filled with the Spirit will exalt Christ more than the

Spirit. Then the work of Jesus is to reveal the Father; he is the unique way to the Father. And in John's gospel we read that the Father glorifies the Son, who will ultimate lay everything at the feet of the Father. What a model of intimate relationships which concentrate on giving to the other!

Many told me how refreshing it was to have talks which fed our minds as well as our hearts and spirits. I came to realize how easily workers overseas develop stultified minds in their Christian experience and this can lead to their feeling distinctly rusty and moribund. We are whole people with hearts, spirits, bodies and minds. Every aspect of our personality needs to develop and grow; otherwise we shall be stunted and out-of-balance in our Christian growth.

Chapter 8

Training For Mission

After less than two years in Malaysia our primary task there was completed and the mission leaders asked us to move to Singapore. We were asked to head up the Orientation Centre, to which all new missionaries from every country came to begin the process of language learning and cultural orientation. In those days they stayed four months in Singapore before moving to the various Asian countries God had called them to.

In OMF we believe in a professional approach to language learning, for without good linguistic ability it will prove impossible to form deep personal relationships and all our teaching and preaching will inevitably appear somewhat foreign and unrelated. In the easier languages one year's full-time study is mandatory, while in the more difficult languages two years' study is expected. Then all missionaries will have an on-going language course with accompanying exams for the next two or three years. Gradually the balance tips from full-time language study with almost no outside ministry towards full-time ministry with little language study.

Much emphasis will be given during those early years to cultural adaptation. How well I remember our constant trouble with the lady who taught Thai! Every term she resigned her job because she said she would not tolerate young missionaries being rude to her and losing their tempers! At first I wondered what was going on and reproved the new workers. Then I discovered that because they made repeated mistakes they became frustrated with themselves and this showed itself in their facial expressions. Such expressions of feeling which are commonplace in the west may seem terribly excessive in Asia.

Each term we invited the first secretary at the Thai Embassy to address our students on Thai culture. Although he had spent many years in Scotland, he still spoke in a Thai manner.

'Did you hear what he said about westerners?' I would ask after he had left.

'He didn't say anything,' was the usual reply. In his indirect Asian manner he had made many quite strong statements, but new workers from the west did not hear what he said. They were just beginning the process of learning.

While we were in charge of the Orientation Centre, the OMF welcomed its first ever Asian members — three workers from the Philippines. Through them we realized afresh how very western OMF really was! For example, our mission centres enjoyed peace and quiet, respecting people's privacy. Our new Asian workers found this eerily silent and longed for more bustle and noise.

One of these first three Asian workers never settled. Local people saw that she looked like them, so assumed that she should know how to behave according to their culture. They therefore had little patience with her when she still spoke the language poorly and made cultural errors. Sadly she could not weather these trials and finally returned home unhappily.

One privilege of the job in Singapore was to attend the central council meetings when all the international leaders of the mission met for a week's discussions. I particularly remember two contributions from our Asian directors.

'OMF is robbing the Singapore churches of God's blessing'. Dr. Chew's untypical, and so shockingly direct accusation shook us all. When we asked what he meant, he explained. 'Jesus said it brings more blessing to give than to receive. OMF with its policy of never asking for money is failing to encourage our churches to give to our missionaries. This robs us of God's blessing through sacrificial giving.'

A week or so later I was asked to speak at a Nurses' Christian Union across the border in Malaysia. I made a point of asking for travel expenses.

The other memorable contribution came after a report on OMF's literature work in Hong Kong, the centre for all our Chinese printing work. The Canadian leader reported that we had been unable to find any local Christian with the necessary business expertise who was willing to take over in leadership and therefore the work was still under missionary direction.

'There are a few Chinese Christians with ability in business', an Asian director interposed with polite understatement. I wondered why we had not been able to recruit such leaders. Was our work structured in such a western fashion that no Chinese could fit in?

Back to Britain

When our time came for home assignment, our mission leaders made it clear to us that they would not want us to return to the Orientation Centre when we came back to Asia. They did not feel we had been satisfactory in this work, while we felt they had not understood us or what we were doing. There were probably mistakes on both sides.

But we went through difficult times. We felt God had definitely called us to this training ministry in Singapore and were convinced our leaders were making a mistake. God's guidance seemed to be frustrated by what we felt was their error, and this combined with our sense of being misunderstood and not appreciated.

The mission assumed we would be happy to return to Indonesia, although it would have to be in Java rather than Sumatra. They did not appreciate that Java is totally different culturally from Sumatra and we might not automatically feel at home there. As we prayed, God caused the words 'you shall not return to this land' repeatedly to come to our attention. These words came in a sermon, in our Bible reading and in a letter from a friend at home. Of course they originally applied to Moses and the people of Israel returning to Egypt, but we knew that God was telling us that he now had other purposes for us besides Indonesia. On our way back to Britain we travelled through America and spoke in various places. As a result we were asked if we would be willing to represent OMF in universities, seminaries and Bible schools. We were in such uncertainty that we felt it right to accept — and then the American leaders decided they really wanted an American for this post.

Month after month slipped by. What was God's next step for us? Satan attacked us with the twin temptations of anxiety and bitterness. We knew it was wrong to yield to either temptation, but sometimes we fell into one or other of these sins. And what cancers they are in the Christian life! We have learned a hard lesson through this and now often counsel fellow-Christians to resist bitterness like a plague.

Then one day I was asked to visit All Nations Christian College in Ware, England. They invited me to speak about Indonesia to the students. I noticed that all the staff attended this talk and was surprised. Afterwards the principal, David Morris, showed me round and talked about his aims in mission training.

'That is very much how I see things', I commented at one stage.

'Then why don't you come and join us'? he replied to my amazement. He immediately suggested that I talk with Elizabeth, bring her to see the college and join the staff. I had not realized he and the staff were watching me during my talk with this in mind.

A few days later another well-known Bible College also asked me to join their staff and this came as God's confirmation that he was leading us into a lecturing and training role. All Nations was concentrating on training missionary candidates, while the other college was a more general Bible College. My calling is to worldwide mission, so it seemed obvious that All Nations was God's place for us.

However, at that time All Nations was just a small college with no great reputation. Although it was about to link up with two ladies' colleges, it was then still for men only — and like many men's establishments it seemed to lack curtains and flowers while enjoying too many practical jokes! I felt (probably wrongly!) that it was culturally a bit rough.

Then I asked advice from an older Christian who was much involved with Christian financial trusts and big business.

'Don't join All Nations', he warned. 'They will be bankrupt within eighteen months and you will be out of a job. They are buying their property and putting up new buildings too, but they don't have the money for it. And in our present financial crisis in Britain there just isn't that sort of money around.'

But the more we consulted with mission leaders and prayed, the more we felt All Nations was God's place for us. And what a privilege it has proved to be! We have enjoyed almost twenty-five years working there and have seen the college grow in numbers, in the quality of its training, in its academic standards and in the high calibre of our students. We have been thrilled to play a small part in training such men and women of God for service overseas and then to see many of them at work in their various countries all over the world.

But it was not easy to leave OMF and Asia, nor to fit back into Britain. Elizabeth particularly felt the wrench, for she had been born and bred within the family of OMF and in China. Before we returned to Britain a good friend of ours had written, 'Don't forget, returning to Britain requires as much cultural adjustment as ever Hudson Taylor experienced when he went to China.'

We realized that he exaggerated somewhat, but still the point was well made. On our first home assignment back in Britain we had stayed for some months with my mother. She became quite worried about us, for she watched us in our relationship together. In our marriage we had adjusted to the traditional patterns of Sumatra, never looked at each other when others were present and never touched each other. Walking along the seaside promenade in Hove together with all the bikini-clad tourists, we walked discreetly with a yard between us! Finally she took me aside and begged me to make it up to Elizabeth, lest our marriage end in disaster! We had to explain why we behaved in this way and realized that we needed to readjust to life in Britain!

When we first started at All Nations I did not find it easy to sit next to a woman — with my more traditional Asian background it seemed almost flirtatious, although I knew that in the British context it would not appear in that light.

All Nations

When we began work at All Nations it soon became apparent how wonderfully God had prepared us for this ministry. It is such a privilege in life to see how God fits the pieces of the jigsaw perfectly into place.

It had seemed strange how God had moved us from country to country during our ten years with OMF, working in four countries in such a short space of time — Singapore, Thailand, Indonesia and Malaysia. But in those years God gave us exposure to all the major religions of the world, so that we could teach about them not only from book knowledge, but also from personal experience. We had worked with followers of traditional religion in Indonesia, Muslims and Buddhists in Thailand; Chinese religionists, Taoists, Buddhists, Confucianists, Hindus and Sikhs in Malaysia as well as Muslims. And of course I am Jewish.

We had also been given wide experience in many sorts of mission work — pioneer evangelism and church planting; mass movements in large churches, where Bible teaching was the key ministry; hospital evangelism in South Thailand; pastoring a small church in Malaysia; work in large cities like Singapore, market towns like Kluang and Kabanjahe, villages in Thailand and also in Sumatra. When speaking about the practice of mission, this allowed us to speak with personal knowledge. We had worked with the whole spectrum of social backgrounds from sophisticated students and graduates to up-country people who lacked the education and material wealth of a city. And in our training work in Singapore we had come to see something of the needs of new missionaries, the next stage after our graduates leave All Nations.

How wisely God leads us step by step without our knowing!

But in coming to All Nations we also had a great deal to learn. We were quite out of touch with all the latest thinking and books on mission. When we accepted the offer of a job there, we were given a pile of books to read — and I remember going home laden with library books. We had the personal experience, but lacked the academic reading, and for the past twenty-five years we have been reading avidly to try to keep abreast of our subjects!

It also proved that our experience was limited. We had some understanding of Asia, but other continents remained a closed book to us. It became a source of great joy to learn about what God was doing in other parts of the world. How much we would have benefited in Asia if we had known more about the churches in Africa and Latin America! All churches and all Christians have so much to learn from each other.

At that stage in the history of All Nations we had several staff members with experience in Africa, but no one from Latin America. I took it on myself to read widely about that continent in order to fill that gap to some extent. After a while I was asked to join the board of the evangelical Anglican South American Mission Society and then did a tour of seven South American countries. I was fascinated to witness the growth of the Pentecostal churches in some countries, to have first-hand experience of Roman Catholic charismatics, to weep with the people of the tragic shanty-towns in their abysmal poverty and hopelessness, to note the first stirrings of worldwide missionary concern in that continent and of course to share with evangelical missionaries and churches.

I have learned to give a heart-felt 'amen' on a Sunday when we remind ourselves in the Creed that we believe in the church. The glory of God's great family world-wide and the huge privilege of belonging to that family beggars description. Now that we have a travelling ministry in many countries we have experienced the reality of that family — brothers and sisters of every race and colour in all countries.

All Nations training principles

It was David Morris' genius which determined the future course of the college. Back in the 1960s he observed that a plethora of Bible colleges filled the niche of training men and women for evangelistic and church ministries within their own countries. All Nations could hardly compete with so many well estab-lished schools which generally did a good job. But he saw that Britain lacked quality cross-cultural mission training colleges. We could fill that specialist corner of the training market; and worldwide mission lay close to David's heart and calling. Unashamedly All Nations has since then specialized in cross-cultural mission, not accepting students wanting to work among their own people in Britain unless it is with ethnic minorities.

a) *Holistic training*

The college aims to integrate Biblical studies, theology, church history and pastoral counselling with cross-cultural studies, the study of other faiths, mission practice, practical church work and down-to-earth courses on tropical hygiene, food production or car maintenance. The spiritual, pastoral, practical and missiological should all interrelate.

This means that we do not want to study scripture merely from a traditional western and gentile viewpoint, but to see the Bible through the eyes of people from other cultures and backgrounds. Likewise church history must not be centred on Europe and North America with occasional sorties overseas by intrepid white missionaries! Church history must include the history of the African and Asian churches, for example. This integrated approach should apply to all subjects without exception.

This sounds easy, but in fact it presents considerable difficulties. Almost all the accepted academic commentaries and theological works stem from traditional western backgrounds and they do not normally relate at all to cross-cultural studies. As soon as academic approaches are stressed, there is an inevitable danger therefore that students will slip into the ethnocentric bias of western gentile academia.

Nor is the balance between good academic standards and practical or spiritual training easy to maintain. I have observed this tension both at All Nations and in other colleges in Britain and elsewhere. Today academic excellence is vitally important in our training, but there is a risk of both staff and students becoming too busy.

Staff may begin to accumulate a multitude of assignments to correct as well as having to prepare their lectures. To keep up-to-date in our subjects requires considerable reading, study and research. Accreditation systems with universities mean all sorts of board meetings, red-tape paper work and the production of long documents concerning the courses offered. This is all quite unavoidable, but it limits the amount of time available for personal care of students. In a bureaucratic and increasingly impersonal world, many of us are asking how we can maintain our very personal, spiritual and practical emphasis.

Students also may develop such a heavy work programme with long hours in the library and sitting in front of the computer, that they too may have no time to work through personal issues or practical questions concerning the work of mission. This problem may arise from the fact that the church worldwide is demanding ever increasing academic qualifications.

b) Tutorial system

The heart of the All Nations training lay in the tutorial system. Each member of staff took responsibility for about twelve students. We saw them regularly on a personal basis, worshipped as a group three times a week, held a weekly discussion time together and often socialized as a tutorial group. Students discussed their work load with their tutor who had considerable input into what courses they followed. The tutor also marked their assignments and could vary the academic level as well as the content of what was expected from their students. This allowed considerable flexibility. We found that this was vitally important, for students going to Japan need different studies from those going to the Muslim world; and students vary both in their academic ability and in how much they already know.

But the primary emphasis of the tutorial system is personal and spiritual. The heart of training for Christian ministry must lie in our relationship with the Lord himself. Without this all academic ability will be in vain. It is a known fact that the main stresses among clergy and missionaries come from unresolved pastoral problems, and once a person is ordained or has gone overseas as a missionary it becomes much harder to deal with these issues. The training college has particular responsibilities in this matter.

During my time at All Nations I felt that this personal and pastoral work was the most important aspect of our calling. Whatever the temptation to cut corners in this area and allow it to be crowded out by other pressing calls, priority needed to be given to this pastoral work. I generally aimed to give about twelve hours a week to individual talks with students.

c) Diversity

David Morris's oft repeated picture of college life was that of an orchestra, each instrument being different and yet all playing together to form beautiful music.

We always looked for new staff to be quite different from any present members. They should have very varied experiences and personalities, bringing new emphases spiritually and biblically. Some of us enjoyed the charismatic renewal of the Holy Spirit, while others related to the Lord in a more reformed tradition. Some strongly insisted on believers' baptism, while others cheerfully baptized their babies. The spectrum of millennial views was represented amongst us. While the socio-political dimension of mission became centre-stage with some of us, with others the focus was on the pressing evangelistic needs of the unevangelized. The role of women and sexism, ecology and speciesism, mission from the two-thirds world — all sorts of emphases attracted the attention of someone!

But students frequently commented on the fact that such diversity in no way induced disharmony. They saw the deep love and unity which reigned amongst us. We wanted to demonstrate by our own model that Christian unity is centred on our loving relationship with Jesus Christ in accordance with scripture. If Jesus Christ, his cross and resurrection are pre-eminent, then we can happily disagree on most other matters.

Both staff and students came therefore from a wide range of denominations, from Pentecostal and newer charismatic churches through to Anglican and Lutheran with everything in between. But we were all evangelical, submitting to the ultimate authority of the Bible and affirming the fundamental credal statements of the Christian church.

With this wide diversity we tried always to emphasize the freedom to worship the Lord in ways which reflected our particular backgrounds. We much enjoyed times of worship which stemmed from African, Latin American or other overseas backgrounds. We encouraged charismatic students and staff to lead worship in that manner; more meditationally inclined people helped us to enjoy their form of worship; those who preferred a more liturgical or traditional free church style were asked to bring their emphasis to us all. All of us were exhorted to centre our worship on Christ, join in fully with the pattern of worship brought to us and learn to enjoy it.

Generally this worked well and we really knew the presence of the Lord in our midst. Occasionally inadequate time was given to preparation and our worship fell into the lowest-common-denominator syndrome, not really having any significant character at all.

Our students, of course, reflect the churches they come from and in our modern day worship styles have become of paramount importance. Christians now seem to find it very difficult to worship in ways which they are not accustomed to or which they would not themselves choose. Indeed we notice around Britain that this has become a very divisive issue in the church. I find this terribly sad and distressing. It is surely a major sin amongst us.

When our graduates go overseas, it is very likely that they will not find local churches which worship in their way. They will have to learn to enjoy new patterns and fit in with them. So we felt it of great importance that at All Nations we should all learn to glorify the Lord and worship him in a wide variety of styles.

Culturally too staff and students reflected a great diversity. I often think back to the first day of one academic year when all the students were standing around somewhat shyly in the main hall below the great staircase. Suddenly a new Greek student who came from a somewhat unsophisticated family in Zaire walked ostentatiously down the stairs on his hands! Unabashed as a new student, he had no hesitation in showing off his skills so dramatically. On arrival at the foot of the stairs he saw a beautiful young Japanese lady in her kimono standing discreetly a yard away from her somewhat traditional Japanese husband. The Greek went straight to her, gave her a large hug and kissed her on both cheeks! The husband's shock was palpable! Both Japanese and Greek had to learn that cultures vary!

Some of our African students were tempted to doubt the spirituality of European students because they spent so little time in prayer and were so undisciplined regarding regular morning times of devotion. Koreans sometimes felt that others prayed so unemotionally and softly that they could not really mean business with the Lord. Some British students demonstrated their freedom in Christ by enjoying a visit to the local pub or having alcoholic drinks in their room, while to many overseas Christians such practices are anathema. Students from poorer backgrounds in the former Central Asia or India did not appreciate the obvious wealth of American or European students with their computers, libraries of CDs etc.

But the college emphasis on our life together as a family remained true. We so enjoyed our relationships as a community and felt we belonged to one another as united members of the body of Christ. As the college grew in numbers and became increasingly busy, we had consciously to struggle to maintain this depth of love together. I personally found it important to work hard at the start of each year to learn the names of each student and then add to the name their basic character, gifts and background. In this way I could relate helpfully to any student who came to see me about personal issues or their guidance about their future calling. Meal-time conversations also often led to useful discussion of this nature.

d) Families

In the past very few colleges really trained students' partners. As a result husbands often did biblical and theological studies, but their wives did not keep pace and were not really able to discuss adequately with their husbands. In this way a chasm could develop within a marriage and the husband might even find that a single lady worker gave him more intellectual satisfaction than his wife. A recipe for disaster!

Both in church life in Britain and also in mission overseas husband and wife should form a team working together. We felt strongly that wives need training just as much as husbands. So we developed a policy that we would not generally accept married applicants to the college unless both partners became students. Of course we had to institute an adequate nursery for their children so that this policy could be practicable.

Still today we are saddened by the fact that many colleges maintain the old-fashioned tradition that partners of clergy or missionaries don't need full training.

'I dread the day when my husband becomes a vicar,'

the young wife of a curate said to us recently. 'I feel terribly inadequate for all that will be expected of me as a vicar's wife.' She had virtually no biblical or theological training, just an occasional practical lecture at the college where her husband had trained.

On the All Nations staff team too we stressed the importance of a proper balance between male and female in approximately equal proportions. We have also felt it important to have married couples with both partners working together as lecturers. In these days where marriage is so under threat, students deeply appreciate the model of a married couple working together. And for ourselves Elizabeth and I have always shared our ministry and we were deeply grateful to be able to work together on the teaching staff at All Nations. When eventually Elizabeth reached the age of retirement, we agreed that both of us should leave the college to move on to new ministries.

e) Leadership patterns

A training college like All Nations requires quite different organizational structures from the normal secular business. The staff team consists of well qualified and very experienced men and women. In other contexts each of us would have been a leader. But in a college situation there is little scope for 'promotion', so each staff member needs to be given ample opportunity to use all their gifts and play an important part in the formation of overall policy in the college.

Although David Morris was undoubtedly the

leader in the college, we very much appreciated his habit of dropping into our studies to discuss things with us personally. In this way he would bounce his ideas off us and we felt we could influence all that was going on in the life of the college. Later principals relied more on staff meetings where college life was discussed and decisions taken. Such consultation processes should prevent staff from feeling marginalized and having no adequate opportunity to feed in their ideas.

From my time at All Nations and my visits to many other colleges around the world I have observed the danger of leadership becoming centralized in the hands of an élite consisting of the principal and one or two others. I have also seen the benefit of involving all the staff at every stage of decision making even if this takes more time.

David Morris not only laid the foundations for the whole future development of the college with its tutorial structure and its holistic approach to mission training, but he also warmly encouraged his staff. From him I have learned the importance of leaders giving their workers the sense that they are deeply appreciated — George Steed also had done this for us in Indonesia. David often told us that the All Nations staff team was the best in any college and that our students were just wonderful! One may smile and say that this was a little naive and unrealistic, but the constant emphasis — and he really believed it(!) — gave us all a warm feeling of being loved, trusted and appreciated. I believe this to be a vital ingredient of all Christian leadership.

Actually it was not difficult to think positively about our students. With more applicants than places each year, we were able to be quite selective. Aged largely between twenty six and the early thirties they were mature; and many had sacrificed well paid jobs in order to give themselves to missionary training and service. Much of our fellowship and friendship revolved around our students.

Living in Stanstead Abbotts

When we came to the college, we were able to have our own house in the local village community. Teaching in a totally Christian institution, it has been helpful to live in a normal English village, attend our local church and be part of ordinary life around us. Now that we no longer work full-time at the college, we so appreciate the fact that we can remain here in the same church and community with many of our long-term friends.

We believe it has also been good for students to see us playing a part in our local church, putting some of our mission principles into practice where God has placed us. We have been richly blessed through the friendship and fellowship of the local church which in the past ten years has become more evangelical. How good it has been to see God at work in people's lives here in Britain too!

Actually we are often away from our home, for over the years God has led us into an increasingly wide travelling ministry both in Britain and overseas. For many years we spent our college vacations ministering in other countries, while two or three weekends a month during term-time saw us holding mission weekends in churches around Britain and in university Christian Unions.

Sometimes our colleagues on the staff at All Nations did not appreciate our wider ministry, feeling we should concentrate on life at All Nations only. It took some while before it was seen that through us God led many people to commit their lives to Christian mission, and some also felt God's call to study at All Nations. Through our overseas work All Nations became better known in other countries of Europe and in Korea. Now it has become well-known all over the world because of the quality of our graduates as well as through visits from various staff members.

We noticed too how our students valued the fact that we had up-to-date experience of so many countries and were also in touch with what was happening in the British church. It is so easy for college staff to lose touch with the world outside, and our mission experience can slip into the distant past as the years go by! For example, our experience in Indonesia is now a considerable number of years behind us and it is vitally important to keep up-to-date.

But when we come home from our travels it is always a special delight to walk or bicycle up the long college drive. In winter the old Victorian building sparkles under a covering of snow and the woods around look beautiful. In the spring drifts of snowdrops are followed by whole carpets of daffodils and then the bluebells begin. Even after so many years at the college these sights still move us as we go through the woods with their rich variety of old trees.

We delight also to return to the warm fellowship of staff and students!

Chapter 9

Insights from a Travelling Ministry

Only half a dozen young people turned up for the church Youth Fellowship, to which I had been invited to speak. They sat around looking somewhat bored. After a while someone half-heartedly introduced me with little sign of enthusiastic expectation — and I spoke!

We had only recently returned to Britain, no one knew us and we were invited largely to rather dreary churches and other small and often lifeless meetings. It was not easy to break through the atmosphere of sleepy traditionalism, but we believed we should give of our best at any meeting we were called to. Often people were shocked into interested wakefulness. Perhaps we should have apologized for disturbing their slumbers!

After that youth meeting one young man asked me if I would be willing to come to his university Christian Union to speak. I was delighted. He came from

Durham University which had a thriving group of several hundred spiritually dynamic and hungry students.

So doors for more significant ministry began to open and invitations to more lively churches, youth and student groups as well as conferences trickled in through our letter-box. After a few years people in other countries began to ask us to speak at their conferences, lecture in Bible schools, preach and teach in churches. In this way God moved us into a world-wide travelling ministry both around Britain and in every continent, and what a privilege this has been!

Knowing that on average we fly each month for ministry overseas, people often ask us whether we enjoy travel. The answer is both 'yes' and 'no'. The actual process of travelling has long since lost its romantic appeal. Many hours spent at Heathrow yield little real pleasure despite our customary pot of coffee while waiting. Our own sitting-room at home is more comfortable than a transit lounge for reading a good book! And long overnight flights to more distant countries with the inevitable jet-lag seem to us a dreary hazard one just has to endure.

But we thoroughly enjoy actually being in the different countries. It is a constant challenge and stimulating pleasure to fit into a wide variety of cultural situations and churches. What an exciting privilege too to witness first-hand the realities of church and mission work all over the world, to see with one's own eyes what God is doing!

We notice how Christian reporting about other countries does not always match the reality. An element of propaganda and bias easily creeps in. Reports stemming from denominational sources often seem to assume that the only churches worth mentioning overseas belong to their denomination. When news of another country is channelled through Christians with strong charismatic leanings, the movements of God seem to double in size and it is evident that God works only through their sort of church. Reformed Christians on the other hand seem to delight in underlining the spiritual blindness which afflicts the world. This emphasis sometimes fails to reflect the joyful thanksgiving which Paul stresses in his letters. When Paul and Barnabas returned to the church in Antioch, they 'declared all that God had done' — not what God had not done! — 'and how he had opened a door of faith to the Gentiles' (Acts 14:27). Positive optimism and thanksgiving without exaggeration should characterize our mission reporting. We need also to give people an overall picture of what God is doing in the world today through churches and missions from different backgrounds. Our aim is to glorify the Lord who is the truth, not our denomination, mission, or theological and spiritual emphasis.

Know God's programme

Once or twice over these past years we have felt our lives becoming overbusy and have needed to discern God's purposes for us. It is so easy to accept all sorts of invitations without learning the vital lesson of saying 'no'. One's ministry can then become cluttered with a multitude of activities, all of which seem good, but the essential purposes of God for us and through us can be watered down.

In such situations I have found it helpful to spend a protracted time alone with the Lord to spread before him all the claims on our time and energy. I like to go somewhere beautiful for a day or half a day in a place where there are no distractions of people, phone, letters or desk. It is then a pleasure to meditate on each of the various claims on our time and consider before the Lord whether he has called us to this particular work, whether he wants us to spend more or perhaps less time on it — or even to give it up altogether.

I remember one such day, sitting on a rock by the sea with an otter preening itself in the water nearby. I considered each area of my life, spending about an hour in silence before the Lord to think about each form of ministry. At the end of the day I knew for certain that God wanted me to resign from one rather prestigious committee and attend another less frequently. He seemed also to underline his call to a wider speaking and to a writing ministry.

At each stage of life all of us have to reconsider what God's programme holds for us — and from time to time it changes and develops.

Keep your promise!

When we were still members of OMF a church asked the mission to supply a speaker for their mission weekend. I was chosen to fulfil this assignment. But then I was asked to speak at a large well-known London church, and this invitation came to me personally, whereas the other request came to the mission. I asked OMF to replace me with another of their workers so that I could accept what I felt to be a more significant opportunity.

But I had already told the first church that I would be with them. They rightly pointed out that I should have kept my promise and not been drawn away by the better known and larger church. They felt hurt that I seemed to denigrate their importance and they were offended.

I learned my lesson. As a Christian my word ought to be trustworthy, for we are called to model our lives on that of Christ himself who lives in us by his Spirit in order to make us holy as he is holy. We trust the words and promises of God, so our words and promises must also be trustworthy.

Sometimes since then I have found myself driving along the motorway, thinking to myself, 'Why on earth did you accept this meeting?' — and I have been tempted to find some excuse not to go! But even if I feel it was a mistake to say 'yes' to the invitation, my promise needs to be honoured. Then comes the urgent prayer: 'Lord, forgive me if I failed to follow your purposes about this meeting. But please overrule my foolishness, fill me with your Spirit and speak through me in ways which will glorify you and bring blessing to this church.'

Beware pride!

'It's a special pleasure and privilege to have . . . . with us today'. Such introductory remarks preface our speaking and preaching again and again. Our coming to that church or conference may also be preceded by leaflets and notices which make us out to be celebrities. And during our time there people entertain us most generously with warm hospitality and first class meals. We are grateful to our hosts for their kindness — it was not always like that in the past! In former years we suffered occasional horrors when coming as visiting speakers.

One well-known evangelical church put me up in a home where the wife was mentally ill. My tiny bedroom had mould on the walls and the bed itself smelled with damp. The little window refused absolutely to open and it was the season of the year when I can be prone to asthma! At breakfast my hostess insisted on serving me repeatedly with fried eggs, bacon, sausage and tomato — I might manage a second helping, but a third, fourth and fifth only guaranteed that the church would receive a 'heavy word' in that morning's sermon!

On another occasion I drove up the ample drive to a large and beautiful home. 'I shall be well looked after here', I thought to myself with rampant materialism.

As bed-time approached, the lady of the house showed me proudly up to my spacious and well-appointed bedroom. 'I've made your bed up on the floor', she beamed with obvious pride in her thoughtfulness.

'I knew you were a missionary, so I know you'll be more comfortable on the floor.'

But in our modern day Christians have learned to treat their visiting speakers with wonderful generosity. The danger now is that we may be raised onto a pedestal and made to feel that we really are special people.

Always received as the honoured speaker and constantly praised, we all face the pressing danger of actually believing what people politely say about us. Pride can take us over and we may begin to think of ourselves as 'the big speaker'.

How important it is that we remain the normal everyday people that we really are! In the Bible meekness and humility hold a central place as God's conditions for his blessing; pride and arrogance destroy a relationship with God and any fruitful ministry.

Keep fresh!

Old age crept up inexorably on Elizabeth's father, who had been a missionary doctor for over thirty years in China. When he got into his nineties he found himself no longer able to get out of the house.

'You must miss your church', I said to him one day when we were talking together.

'Not really', he replied after a pause. 'The brothers and sisters are very kind and visit me frequently, so I get plenty of fellowship.'

He stopped and looked searchingly at me. After a short while he continued, 'You see, I've heard it all before', a statement which made considerable sense as he had been a Christian for over eighty years by then! He then added with a twinkle in his deep-set old eyes, 'Many times!'

With his sharp mind he continued to think deeply to the end of his long life, and his words challenged me. Would people say of my preaching and teaching, 'We've heard it all before — many times'?

I determined not just to regurgitate hackneyed old teaching, but keep myself fresh in the knowledge of God and his word. After all, God is infinitely greater than anything any of us has fathomed thus far, so surely we can reach out to fresh reality without denying the foundations of old truths. And the Bible as God's word holds treasures beyond what we have thus far mined.

In this context I had already noticed the danger of too much thematic preaching, in which the speaker determines what he or she wants to say and uses Bible verses to support it. With our limited human capacity such teaching can become terribly repetitive. But regular and systematic Bible exposition forces us to new insights and emphases.

In looking at scripture through Jewish eyes I have found God speaking in ways which are somewhat different from traditional gentile understanding. This has helped me in keeping fresh in my study of the Bible.

Then too I have found it helpful to reverse the accepted pattern of Bible reading, in which we are encouraged to interpret so-called difficult passages in the light of what is clear. I have sometimes started with the apparently obscure sections or what seem to me unexplained anomalies. I believe that the biblical writers were men of good sense who wrote logically and intelligently, so there must be a reason for those obscure or anomalous passages.

So I began my study of Romans by asking why chapters 9–11 follow the earlier chapters and lead into the final section of the book. This led me to see Paul's emphasis on the universality of the Christian faith, both for Jews and gentiles because justification is by faith and not by the Law of Moses which is fundamentally for Israel.

In John's gospel I saw that the desire of the Greeks to see Jesus was the final sign in the lead-up to the climactic sign and word of the cross and resurrection in chapters thirteen to the close of the book. It seemed such an insignificant event, just a few Greeks wanting to see him, and Jesus' response seems quite out of proportion — 'the hour has come for the Son of man to be glorified' (Jn. 12:23). The Old Testament vision of the gentiles being drawn in to Zion to worship the God of Israel was now fulfilled — the gentile Greeks came to Jesus, the God of Israel and Zion incarnate. John is showing how Jesus is the final climax of all that is positive in the Old Testament, including God's universal purposes for all nations.

It is my prayer that in various ways God will preserve me from merely mouthing old truths without going further into his revelation of himself.

'Lord, please keep me fresh — for myself and for my teaching of others.'

A wide ministry

While I deeply respect those who specialize in one area of study and of ministry, I feel God has led me into a wide ministry.

The Lord has allowed me the privilege of preaching and teaching in churches of very different backgrounds. Although I am an Anglican myself, doors have been opened to me into churches of other denominations — Baptist, Brethren, Pentecostal, New Church etc. In Britain I deeply appreciate the rich biblical contribution of the churches associated with Proclamation Trust while at the same time we have enjoyed the dynamic vitality and vision of the Pioneer People churches. As long as Jesus Christ is uplifted as pre-eminent and the foundational truths of the Christian faith are upheld, I feel at home. I want constantly to reaffirm that our unity together lies in our relationship to Christ — after all, it is in Jesus Christ that we find salvation and spiritual life; everything else must remain secondary, however important it may be.

In different circles we have become known for teaching on various subjects — Jewish issues, Islam and Muslim mission, mission theology and our attitude to other faiths, the practice of mission and church planting, biblical exposition and spiritual encouragement. We very much enjoy this rich variety of topics on which we are asked to teach. When teaching at All Nations I also had the joy of lecturing on many different subjects in relation to Christian mission and to other faiths.

In our travelling ministry we are also invited to very different forms of ministry. In some countries we lecture in seminaries and Bible colleges, while in others we have the privilege of helping to train missionary candidates. Overseas we sometimes minister within the national church, but on other occasions we are called to serve at the annual conference of an expatriate mission. Missionary weekends in churches are interspersed with mission conferences, university Christian Union meetings, clergy gatherings etc. And what a joy it is to be allowed to expound the scriptures and to teach in such a variety of contexts!

Sometimes we notice that width of ministry gives insights which may be missed by those whose focus is narrower, although of course width inevitably prevents the depth which comes from specialization. But by avid reading over many years we try to avoid the shallow ignorance which can come from too much width. My membership of the Fellowship of European Evangelical Theologians from its inception gave me the added stimulus of good relationship with leading evangelical theologians all over Europe.

Before turning to look at a few of the countries where we have been allowed to minister, I want to emphasize one other tremendous privilege God has given us. In most of our travels overseas and much of our work in Britain too Elizabeth and I have had the joy of working together as a team. As I have already said, we complement each other with our very different personalities and ministry styles and we have specialized in different subjects, but they interrelate. We pray that in our service together we may encourage other married couples as well as being a model of the teaching role both of men and women. Of course there are a few churches which reject this model and we have to be prepared to adjust accordingly. We would not wish to force our own views on others, but only to serve — and yet, when we are allowed to minister together, we often find that people see the value of it.

Mission congresses

Although invited to the watershed missions congress in Lausanne in 1974, I had already agreed to do a Bible teaching tour of Sarawak and Sabah in East Malaysia. But I gained my first experience of such a world congress in Pattaya, Thailand in 1980. This international missions conference was organized by the Lausanne Movement. It was located in a plush five-star hotel by the beautiful sea-side in a scenic but seedy tourist centre. With sensitive forethought the manager sent the hotel's prostitutes away for a week's holiday during our consultations!

The gathering of a large crowd of evangelical leaders from all around the world gives the Christian faith more of a public image and helps our voice to be heard. It was a great joy to meet and talk with godly men and women from a wide variety of countries and situations. Many new links and friendships were forged during those days. Particularly those of us involved in Jewish mission in Britain met up with the American Jews for Jesus for the first time. This led to a close fellowship and cooperation from then on, and finally to Jews for Jesus beginning work in Britain too. At Pattaya Jewish mission took a giant step forward and for this reason

I am deeply grateful as I think back to that consultation.

On the first day all the Christians met together in order to get to know each other. I was interested to hear about half of us saying, 'I became a believer through another Jewish Christian's witness.' But the others of us testified that it was gentile Christians who had brought us to faith in Jesus Christ. Both Jewish and gentile Christians can play a vital part in witness among Jews.

But it has to be said that most of the debates and even the major papers were rather inadequate and disappointing. Pragmatic business methodology pushed biblical theology and missiology into the sidelines. I remember one Scandinavian theologian leaving the hall after a main address and saying to me, 'What's the difference between marketing the gospel and marketing Coca Cola?'

I had to agree with him that in the paper we had just listened to, words like 'God' or 'gospel' could easily have been replaced by 'Coca Cola' without altering the basic sense of the talk.

In general I felt that three lobbies were represented, none of which really heard the others. From the platform came the strongly pragmatic approach to mission associated with the Californian church-growth school. Strong opposition to this came from a more left-wing emphasis on the socio-political dimension of mission which stressed the need for holistic approaches. Less vocal and therefore hardly noticed, some leading theologians from Scandinavia plus a few others longed for a more biblical orientation with a strong evangelical theology. Sadly the structure of the congress allowed an unfortunate polarization of views to evolve.

Some years later the second Lausanne Congress took place in Manila. I was particularly pleased to be able to attend this gathering not only for its own sake, but also because I had never previously visited the Philippines. My original missionary call had seemed to be to the Philippines, but God had redirected me to other countries, so it was exciting finally to see that country.

At Manila it was encouraging to see that the tremendous growth of the charismatic renewal worldwide was finally recognized. It was now welcomed as an integral part of the whole evangelical movement and was well represented on the platform. I noticed too that the more biblical wing of the Roman Catholic Church was also edging towards acceptance, although this causes very considerable disquiet in the Latin American and South European lands where evangelicals have been badly persecuted by that church. A Russian Orthodox priest was also warmly welcomed onto the platform and given loud applause. Some of us were particularly pleased that a lady from Jews for Jesus was allowed to share her testimony in a main meeting — it is exceedingly rare that a Jewish Christian is invited to speak at a major Christian congress of this nature. We could wish that at some stage a Jewish Christian might be asked to expound the scriptures in a world Christian conference — after all, the Bible was written by Jews!

Between Pattaya and Manila considerable development of thought had taken place. At the Manila conference the social dimension of mission was unhesitatingly assumed. Christian workers involved in alleviating the sufferings of the poor, the despised and the oppressed were warmly applauded.

Both at Pattaya and at Manila the undue domination of American delegates caused some resentment. Some of us also felt that as participants we were just there to give weight to the conference statement drawn up by the leadership.

Again for me the chief value of the conference lay in the new personal friendships and relationships formed there — as well as many former ones being renewed and strengthened. But generally I became very much aware that such conferences are really not my scene; because of the shallow input and inadequate discussion they leave me frustrated and I have determined that I shall not attend another world conference of this nature as a delegate.

Evangelical-Roman Catholic Dialogue on Mission (ERCDOM)

From 1977–1984 John Stott and Monsignor Basil Meeking, until recently bishop of Christchurch in New Zealand, led a series of dialogue conferences in which I participated.

Stott had realized the danger of evangelical Christians holding an out-of-date stereotyped view of Roman Catholics and wished that we could appreciate the contemporary position as seen by Catholics themselves. At the same time leading Roman Catholics had come to see that the large majority of Protestant missionaries do not belong to the ecumenical movement centred in Geneva in the World Council of Churches. Although the WCC claims to represent Protestantism, actually in international mission the majority of active missionaries are evangelical and do not adhere to the WCC. So the Roman Catholics wanted to penetrate beyond pejorative terms like 'fundamentalist' and find out where we stand. At our first gathering in Venice they were surprised to discover that we were theologically and missiologically quite well grounded, for they had imagined us to be pragmatic practitioners without much academic weight. And we found that our Reformation-based views of the Roman Catholic Church had become somewhat out-dated — *aggiornamento*, the evolution of faith and practice, had carried the church considerably further.

Inevitably in dialogue one's own understanding of the Christian faith is challenged. I had always been taught that new birth and conversion lead into and are followed by our belonging to the church of God. This sequential view changed under the critical scrutiny of our Catholic friends. I realized the simple truth that relationship to God in Christ by the Spirit goes hand-in-hand together with belonging to his body, the church. If we are converted to God, we automatically become part of his church — like a baby which is born not only as child of its parents, but also simultaneously into a wider family. The joys and burdens of aunts, uncles and cousins fall unavoidably on its shoulders. So I gained a new view of the absolute importance of the fact that all Christians must be part of the church.

Some of our Catholic friends faced in a new way the question of authority. Where does the ultimate authority lie? Is it in the church as Christ's body or in scripture as Christ's revealed word?

In these conferences both sides learned much. But perhaps the greatest benefit came from developing good friendships on a personal level. Such face-to-face sharing allowed a much deeper penetration into the heartbeat of the other community.

Conclusion

In this chapter we have seen some lessons God has tried to teach me as a necessary background to a travelling ministry. Then too the reader has joined me at two world congresses and one series of dialogue conferences. Such meetings play a part in the overall work of mission, but personally God has called me to concentrate on the hands-on work of mission around the world. I fear that too much kudos attaches to those who spend much of their time and energy in international consultations and conferences, but God is looking for those who get their hands dirty in the down-to-earth work of preaching the gospel and teaching the church. There is a danger that many of our most gifted Christian leaders may devote too much time to such high-profile gatherings and the work of mission be robbed of their active contribution.

Chapter 10

A Whistle-Stop World Tour

With the previlege of a travelling ministry many impressions and lessons flood our minds. In this chapter I want to pick out just a few.

Israel

Plump middle-aged European tourists in Bermuda shorts dancing to Israeli music in celebration of Jewish festivals; crowds of foreigners thronging ornate Roman Catholic or Orthodox churches at biblical sites; brown-habited Franciscan monks carrying a large wooden cross as they lead a procession down the Via Dolorosa or kneel piously for prayer in the middle of the street; camera-clicking visitors attending a Sabbath or Sunday messianic congregation in order to get a picture of 'genuine Jewish Christians'. With such an image of Israel today I had no desire to visit that land.

Then a German former student of ours heard that I had never been to Israel. She was shocked, for she had gone several times. Without my knowing it, she began to pray that the Lord would send her the money to pay for us as a family to visit Israel. Soon afterwards a distant relation died, unexpectedly left her some money in her will, and out of the blue we received a cheque designated to that end.

We thoroughly enjoyed a lovely family holiday in Israel, fascinated to see the very places where biblical events took place. Little details like the topography and distances from one place to another came to life in a new way. We felt we could picture the Bible stories much more easily.

But it was a struggle spiritually. The Wailing Wall particularly, a holy place to all Jews, drew me with a demonic fascination and I found myself going back there again and again. I found it impossible to pray there in the name of Jesus Christ as long as I associated myself with my own Jewish people — to be fully Jewish and to pray in the name of Jesus seemed spiritually impossible. Much prayer was required before I could break this satanic binding.

I also found it hard to reconcile a Christ-like character with the culture of Israel. Israeli life is overtly aggressive, while in the character of Jesus a gracious meekness goes together with his very direct words and actions which sometimes appear quite offensive. I struggled to know how to combine these apparently contradictory characteristics.

This relates also to evangelism among Jews in any country. If we are to relate culturally, very direct methods will be required. The softly-softly British approach with its frequent use of words like 'perhaps', 'rather' or 'somewhat' will not impress. The up-front style of the very Jewish mission Jews for Jesus will cause all sorts of controversy and even violence, but it will cut ice among Jews. It is interesting to see how some gentile churches in Britain would dearly like to push Jews for Jesus into a compromised form of evangelism which suits British churches better.

In the heated controversy about the validity of evangelizing Jews, evangelistic Christians have been accused of 'targeting' Jews. The word 'target' has gained a definitely pejorative significance. This is of course ridiculous, for all teaching or preaching should target people. Sunday Schools target children; women's groups target women; preachers should have in mind what sort of audience they are targeting; even authors are always asked by publishers what sort of readership we are aiming at, which is just another word for 'target'!

Since introducing Jews for Jesus into Britain I have become very aware of how different American Jews are from British or other Jews. We have had to work hard to adapt the American Jewish approach to our British scene, and yet we do not want to water down the highly effective and well-tried patterns of work which have been developed in America.

When I was younger, there were very few mature senior Jewish Christians in Britain, and the few who were well-known we respected as patriarchs among us.

It has been good in these past years to see the growth of messianic Christianity, so that now we have a large number of mature Jewish Christians.

Another struggle I have faced concerns the establishment of messianic congregations. I used to oppose the formation of such ethnic churches, feeling the biblical importance of our unity in Christ across all racial, cultural, class or age barriers. And I still feel it vitally necessary that the church demonstrates this oneness in the Lord; our fractured society desperately needs such a testimony.

But I have come to see that messianic congregations can play a vital role in showing that Jews can become Christians and still maintain their Jewish identity. So many people assume that the church of God is gentile and that Jews cannot be Christians while still remaining truly Jewish. For example, the very name of the ecumenical and anti-evangelistic Council of Christians and Jews assumes that Christians are not Jews, and that Jews are not Christians! The growth of messianic congregations gives the lie to this error. I have been encouraged to see the steady increase in such Jewish churches both in Israel and in other countries. Interestingly, some forty percent of their members are gentiles, so the inter-racial harmony of the gospel of Christ is demonstrated.

In more recent years a new movement has mushroomed. Jews from the former Soviet Union are extremely open to the gospel and large numbers are becoming Christians both in the former Soviet Union, in Israel and in other countries. This has led to considerable growth in the whole messianic movement worldwide.

Some evangelical Christians have received prophecies about the in-gathering of Russian Jews to the land of Israel, but sometimes I wonder whether these prophecies have been adequately discerned. It has led to some Christians dedicating their energies, prayer, time and money to the work of bringing Jews out of Russia, Ukraine and other ex-Soviet lands. Is this a typically satanic ruse to side-track Christians, tempting them to concentrate on what may be good but is of secondary importance? Jesus Christ and salvation in him is the most significant gift we can offer to the Jewish people. Our energies should be focused primarily on evangelism, not on these lesser matters.

In my experience Jewish people in the former Soviet Union show tremendous openness to the good news of Jesus Christ, but after a year or two in Israel or in western countries they gradually become more secular in their thinking and less interested in the gospel. In ex-Soviet countries Jewish Christians may be relatively poor, but they play important roles in the church. However, in Israel, America or Britain they lose self-confidence because culturally they seem less advanced. As a result, their input into the life of the church and its witness is diminished. They become second-class citizens, can't get good jobs and discontent easily overtakes them. We may not be doing them a service when we encourage them to leave the former Soviet Union to move to Israel.

But whatever secondary ministries we may engage in, let us concentrate on bringing the good news of Jesus Christ to Jewish people! That is our primary calling for the good of our Jewish friends and for the glory of the name of Jesus Christ.

Africa

Of all the continents sub-Saharan Africa remains the one I have visited least. But various significant incidents come into my mind when I think of that part of the world and I am deeply grateful to God for the great joy I have experienced in sharing something of the vibrant life of African brothers and sisters. Surely this exuberant spirituality is black Africans' major contribution to the rest of us in God's church worldwide.

As I write this, my mind goes back to an evangelistic outreach in a large marquee in South Africa. Before the meeting we met with the leaders for prayer. Elizabeth humbly took a back seat while the men talked, for she had become accustomed to such approaches when we were in Asia and assumed a similar cultural adaptation here in Africa too. The large Zulu evangelist with dynamic out-going warmth put his hand on her knee and encouraged her: 'Sister, relax and feel free.' And she did!

In Kenya God gave me new insights through talking with a strongly evangelical bishop. 'Evangelical missionaries today have the same doctrine as pre-Reformation Roman Catholics had', he declared provocatively. When asked to explain what he meant, he added significantly, 'Pre-Reformation Catholics held to an infallible dogma which they then tried to use scripture to support. Evangelical missionaries likewise teach an infallible doctrine which they then use the Bible to support. The only difference is that the Roman Catholics call it "dogma" while the evangelicals call it "doctrine". But for both no one is allowed to query their teaching. And the Bible becomes a mere tool to underline and support their teaching.'

As evangelical Christians we actually believe in theory that the Bible as God's word stands above our doctrine, beliefs and experience. These must always be submitted to the test of scripture. But do we believe this in practice?

God used that interview to show me the importance of distinguishing between God's revelation and our theology and practice. We believe that God's word is absolute truth, but our human attempt to understand his revelation, to formulate it theologically, to express it in our teaching and to practice it in our Christian lives — that is human and fallible. Of course we all have much to learn from the history of the church in its theological struggles and in its development of spiritual life and mission; but the church remains human despite the indwelling of the Spirit of truth. We still see only through a glass darkly (1 Cor. 13:12).

In more recent years I have worked a good deal with the whole question of our Christian attitude to other faiths.* In that context Christians are compelled to acknowledge that we have things to learn from other religions and their followers, challenging our understanding of the Bible and our application of God's revealed truth in our everyday lives. And yet in the word of God incarnate and written we have absolute truth.

In each of the black African countries to which we

(For further reading see M. Goldsmith, *What about other Faiths?* Hodder 1989).

have been invited we have been saddened by the divisive problem of tribalism. I recognize that as Europeans we are not in a position to criticize this sin, for ethnic nationalism is rampant in Europe and racism dogs our cultures. Nevertheless we have been grieved to see how tribalism causes many difficulties in the life of the church. Considerable importance is given to the tribal background of church leaders who may be chosen because they belong to the right tribe rather than because they are God's person for the job. Each tribal area may want its own Bible school rather than combining to form one more worthwhile school. Churches themselves can divide along tribal lines. We need to re-emphasize New Testament teaching. Jewish and gentile Christians became deeply united; principles are given on how such racially mixed churches can live together in God's peace.

In East Africa we also observed the danger of undue foreign domination with financial string-pulling. We gave some lectures in a well-known theological school and then drank coffee with the African principal. After some while he shared with us that his views on polygamy and on the millennium differed from those held by the mission which controlled the school.

'But you're the principal', I naively objected. 'Surely you can openly teach what you feel is in line with scripture.'

'Not at all', he said. 'If the mission discovered what I believe on those subjects, either they would force me to resign or they would stop giving financial support to the school — and we are dependent on their money.'

'So our teaching depends on money, not on the Bible', I laughed with sadly sardonic humour.

In another Bible school I asked how their African context influenced the syllabus in biblical studies, theology and church history. To my horror the principal replied, 'In no way! Calvin is the truth. His substitution of Calvin for Christ meant that Africa had nothing to add to western understanding of the Bible. When I returned to All Nations, I introduced a new course on non-western theologies. This was in 1973; it was probably the first course in non-western contextualization in Britain.

Various visits to South Africa have left an abiding impression on my life. I was challenged by a simple African woman who lived in a sprawling shanty-town of tents. Each morning she welcomed a crowd of children to her simple tent home, sang Christian songs with them and told them a Bible story. With little education and inadequate Bible teaching herself she showed the love of Christ to many young people. If she could do this, surely many in our relatively well-taught churches and spacious homes could do likewise!

But the fearful poverty and racial discrimination in the years of apartheid combined with the churches' struggles to relate the biblical gospel to racial, political and social issues. In our areas of Asia we had not been forced to confront such questions, but our visits to South Africa moved us to develop a more holistic faith.

We have clearly appreciated the warm hospitality and natural beauty which are so much a part of South African life. Multi-racial student conferences have blessed us richly, although we have agonized with the participants in the inevitable tensions which came through living closely together during the conference.

In one such conference we asked the students to pretend that they came from a different race, to hear and read the Bible therefore through different spectacles. It was fascinating to hear their testimonies at the close. Many shared how they had never seen the scriptures like that before and God spoke to them in new ways.

One conference was held across the border in Lesotho. On the South African side the fields were yielding abundant crops, while across the border over-grazing caused fearful soil erosion. Wealth and power were measured by how many head of cattle people possessed, so all advice to reduce the numbers of cattle in order to improve their quality and to stop erosion was in vain.

'You must visit my old friend in Lesotho', my old father-in-law said before I went there. 'He is an Anglican clergyman; with whom I've corresponded for fifty years, but we've never actually met.'

Someone kindly drove me out to a remote little village to visit the Canon. On arrival we found this hoary-headed retired man smoking a pipe outside his little African house. When he heard that I was married to his old friend's daughter, he rejoiced and gave me a great hug. Then he went indoors, returning with a book covered in brown paper. The pages were beginning to fall out.

'Your father-in-law sent me this book back in the 1920s', he told me. 'I have asked every Anglican clergyman in Lesotho to read it ever since. It is such a tremendous book.'

It was an old copy of Roland Allen's *Missionary methods: St. Paul's or ours?*, a classic work on indigenous missionary methodology.

Another African country to impress me deeply has been Mali. Although I never got to Timbuktu which had been a dream of mine, it was good to see the beautiful Senegal River flowing through the southern edge of the Sahara region. Brightly coloured women's dresses with one shoulder uncovered added to the cheerful feel of the streets and markets despite the ever-present sand. Women openly washing clothes and bathing half-undressed in the river next to the road made it easy to forget that this was a Muslim country.

I had been invited to speak at a conference for the workers of the Red Sea Mission Team. Knowing that a Norwegian mission with which we have close connections also worked in West Mali, I suggested that the two missions share the conference together. The Norwegians were at that time fairly new to work among Muslims, while the RSMT has worked in Muslim countries throughout its history. But Mali presented RSMT with a new experience for here they were seeing fruit for their labours and churches were emerging. In the Red Sea area where they had traditionally worked such success did not come their way. On the other hand the Norwegians had always worked among tribal peoples in India and had been strongly church-based. Both missions had plenty they could learn from each other.

In the capital city of Bamako I was invited to speak to a group of about fifteen Muslim teachers of the Qur'an in a friend's home. Behind the men sat the grown-up daughter of one of them. She was an enthusiastic Christian. Her glittering eyes sparkled and her mouth split into a bright smile each time she felt these men received a word which drew them one step closer to faith in Christ.

Remembering my experience in other countries in work among Muslims, I was careful to be very polite and diplomatic. I spoke positively about Jesus Christ, but avoided anything negative about Islam.

'Tell us about the errors you feel there are in the Qur'an', they kept begging me. 'And tell us what was wrong with Muhammad and why you don't believe he was a prophet.'

I pointed out that I was only a guest and did not want to speak negatively about their faith. As our time together drew towards a close, their leader thanked me warmly and then remarked. 'The only weakness about this evening has been that you have not told us adequately why we should not believe in Muhammad or the Qur'an. We really want to know that.'

In other countries I had never experienced that sort of desire, so my approach had not been direct enough. As a result, I spoke again after their leader had thanked me. 'As you push me to tell you what I feel to be the weaknesses of Islam, Muhammad and the Qur'an, I am happy to try to fulfil your desire', and I shared with them in that way. They were so pleased! Never before nor since have I shared in a meeting with Muslims of that nature — even after years of mission service, new experiences challenge our flexibility and adaptability.

In Mali I struggled again with the Christian approach to polygamy and marriage. Successful monogamous marriage depends on husband and wife enjoying the companionship of each other. But in traditional Muslim marriage men relate socially with other men and women with women. If the church wants to move its members into monogamy, we have to help people to enjoy companionship and friendship between husband and wife.

It was in Mali that I first realized that slavery is not yet a thing of the past. Across the border in Mauretania a slave market operated even as late as 1979, so still today there are many slaves in that part of the Muslim world.

Latin America

Having ministered in seven South American republics, it is hard to decide which of the many experiences to highlight.

The lady sitting next to me in the plane was fragrantly scented and immaculately coiffured. She asked me what my work was and I replied that I am a missionary. As a traditional Roman Catholic this in no way fazed her.

'What order do you come from?', she asked, 'Jesuit, Franciscan . . . ?'

'No, I'm an evangelical', I replied, using the common word for any Protestant.

A long pause ensued and she looked reflectively out of the window. Then came the words, 'Well, I've never met one of those before.'

Feeling like a two-humped camel in a zoo, I realized the need for an evangelical witness among the upper classes in South America. So many of the churches reach the poorer segments of society, but few can touch the highly sophisticated.

Sometimes people in Britain criticize the South American Mission Society for its rather upper class schools in Chile and Paraguay, but actually they are strategic and they can introduce the gospel to an unevangelized class of people.

While in Chile it was stimulating to interact with Alf Cooper, a graduate of All Nations and a singularly enthusiastic and gifted evangelist with SAMS. One Sunday morning I preached in a church he had planted in a shanty-town area — it was highly informal with no Anglican liturgy. Then in the afternoon he led the service in an upper-class congregation he had started. This time he was smartly dressed in a suit and 'dog collar', the service seemed quite formal and traditional, and yet the gospel came across clearly. Alf had learned not to allow his own preferences to stop him adapting the outward forms of the church to local needs.

Alf has developed a wide ministry of marriage enrichment weekends, meeting the tremendous need evidenced in much of South American society. Through these weekends many come to know the Lord and grow in him. Seeing the Latin tendency to shallow faith, he has also strongly stressed biblical discipling through theological extension courses. So he gives us a model not just of gifted enthusiasm, but also of prayerful adaptation to local situations.

It was a privilege in Peru to attend a Roman Catholic charismatic meeting. During the meeting all worship and prayer was addressed to 'the Lord', but the notices were centred on the Virgin Mary.

In discussion with the leaders afterwards it became clear that they had not realized this development. 'I suppose it's because charismatic prayer is to the Father through the Son by the Holy Spirit', one of them mused, 'and, after all, salvation comes through Jesus, not through Mary.'

I agreed! Clearly the Holy Spirit was leading this church to a proper biblical emphasis, but remnants of their old traditional approaches lingered in the church notices. Hopefully the discussion we had together will have helped promote the developing work of the Spirit of truth.

I was fascinated to discover that in Venezuela the majority of Pentecostal pastors claim to have the gift of tongues, but few have a healing gift. On the other hand, in Chile all will have the gift of healing while many do not have the gift of tongues. It seems that the Holy Spirit gives his people those gifts which the situation demands. In Venezuela medical care was better developed and the gift of healing less essential. But in Chile the poor could hardly afford a visit to the doctor, let alone the medicines prescribed. The gift of healing becomes of vital importance.

The working of the Holy Spirit will vary from one situation to another and even from one culture or generation to another. But he will always exalt the name of Jesus Christ, leading his people into holiness and truth.

The great Brazil for Christ Pentecostal Church seats 35,000 people in its congregation plus a further thousand on red and blue seats on the pulpit. Beneath the pulpit eight fountains with fluorescent pink, green and yellow lights add colour to the hangar-like building. The baptistry lies at the foot of the end fountain with its water cascading down three layers of pink-brown rock. The pastor informed me that one of the church's problems is getting new converts out of the water after baptism — in a hot climate the cool fountain is delightful!

Why should not churches enjoy beauty of this sort?

Asia

The word 'Asia' evokes rich memories of the countries we worked in and many others we have visited. The glorious mountains of Nepal provide a wonderful backdrop to the fast-growing churches, the excellent developmental work of missionaries and the sensational, but grubby Hindu architecture. On one visit there I met some seventy All Nations graduates — it is strange how some countries seem to attract our people more than others.

The godly and sacrificial mission work of Indian missions to the different peoples of their vast country cannot but challenge us comfortable westerners. Huge throngs of people, absolute poverty alongside considerable wealth, gorgeous vivid colours and smells, corruption and chaos — the life of India captures the heart.

Asia is so diverse! The disorder and poverty of Muslim Bangladesh seems a million miles away from progressive Taiwan or the frenetic wealth of Hong Kong. The Roman Catholic Philippines can hardly be compared with Muslim Pakistan or sleepy Laos. But I want to share only a deeply impressive experience in East Malaysia and my knowledge of the great churches of Korea.

My first visit to Sarawak and Sabah was just after the outbreak of revival among the tribal peoples in 1974.

On one internal flight the hard-bitten oil executive next to me waxed eloquent when I told him where I was heading. He had visited that area for a holiday, staying in the government bungalow. The first morning a servant came to wake him at five o'clock, insisting that everyone always goes to the morning prayer meeting. My then non-Christian New Zealand friend was shocked — he was not accustomed to going to prayer meetings early in the morning when on holiday! But the servant insisted — and he had to go! He did not understand the language, but was soundly converted that morning.

Some people walked three days to get to our teaching meetings, and then three days home again. In a revival situation I saw the colossal need for good Bible teaching, otherwise the revival will die out with candy-floss superficiality. In one area the whole population had come into renewed life in Christ. Only one couple resisted the movement of the Spirit, and they became almost a tourist attraction! People constantly pointed them out, saying 'Those are the non-Christians' or, 'That's where the non-Christians live'! A new holiness swept through the area. The Muslim government withdrew all police as they were now redundant. At the end of my stay, because my flight was delayed, I left my suitcase unattended in the airport hall for three days with my camera loose on top. When I returned, the suitcase and camera stood safely there with masses of little brown envelopes lying on it. These were thank-offerings for the Bible teaching and they contained enough money to cover my airfare from London and back plus all my expenses in Malaysia. I would not recommend this at Heathrow! The impact of revival honesty on our economy in Europe would be enormous!

Over the past ten years we have been visiting Korea regularly. Like many visitors there we have been moved by the deep spirituality of the Christians, their fervent prayerfulness, their passionate worship of the Lord, their spirit of humble service and their deep desire to be fully holy. We feel at home in the main churches of Korea which are reformed Presbyterian, for they have a combination of orderly formality and passionately emotional prayer.

Most western Christians know only of the one huge Pentecostal Church in Seoul which is led by Cho Yong Gi. It is indeed the largest church in the world with several hundred thousand people on a Sunday. Nevertheless some eighty percent of Korean Christians are found in Presbyterian Churches. Since 1905 the Korean churches have grown phenomenally, but sadly growth ground to a halt around 1990 and we need to pray for it to recommence. Meanwhile almost twenty-five per cent of Koreans are now Christian.

We have been impressed by the massive passion for

worldwide mission. The Korean churches are sending large numbers of workers all over the world, and their numbers increase sharply every year. We see here a very influential impetus for world mission. Latin Americans, Africans and other Asians are also now sending growing numbers of missionaries to other countries, but Korea outdoes them all.

But mission from Korea is still relatively new. The need for cross-cultural training stares one in the face, for Korea is a strongly mono-cultural society. We believe that the most strategic task for foreign missionaries in Korea today lies in the training of their missionary candidates. We need also to teach local pastors what overseas mission really means, for they sometimes put undue pressure on their members overseas. They may expect their missionary to lead people to Christ every week and plant churches right from the start of their time abroad — and this may not be realistic in a Muslim context! Pastors can also forget that it takes time to learn a language.

In Britain Christians form such a small minority of our population that we have to try to make the gospel fit the prevailing non-Christian culture. In Korea they are so large and strong that they may be able to form the future culture. Time will tell whether this proves successful or not — the power of non-Christian media and music from abroad is awesome.

As a British Christian one cannot but be impressed by worship meetings in stadiums and churches with tens of thousands of people. This of course requires a different homiletic, for the way we speak in smaller meetings does not relate well to such large gatherings.

But how we long for the day when the Spirit of Christ will sweep through our western nations too!

The ex-communist world

The velvet revolution had just taken place in Czechoslovakia. The huge crowds in Wenceslas Square had seen two secret policemen filming the demonstrations and had dragged them onto the platform. It looked as if they would be lynched, until a Christian minister stepped forward and called everyone to pray the Lord's Prayer. The whole crowd kneeled on the wet ground. So the new era began with prayer, not in bloodshed.

Three months later a smartly dressed middle-aged man spoke with me after a meeting. He spoke several languages and was obviously very well-educated. When asked about his job, to my surprise he replied that he was unemployed.

'Until the revolution I was professor of atheism, but now Marxist atheism is discredited. Nobody can believe that any more,' he explained. 'That's why I've come to the church tonight.'

Then he asked whether Christianity offered an adequate ideology for the modern world. What difference would it make to industry, if we all became Christians? What difference to education, to medicine, to politics. . .?

Thinking people in ex-communist lands are not looking for an escapist spiritual gospel which touches only our personal lives, but also for an ideology which can underlie every side of life in today's society. After

the all-embracing ideology of Marxism they face both
a spiritual and ideological vacuum.

Such openness has allowed all sorts of churches and
missions to reap a harvest. Western Christians have
exported all our divisions and new churches of all sorts
have sprung up — extreme charismatic, anti-
charismatic, various millennial views, fundamentalist,
evangelical etc. Different Korean missions have also
added their denominations. The pre-revolution
Christians in these countries look on in bewilderment.
Why can we not work under existing churches to help
them plant new congregations? I know many of the
former churches were legalistic, but they have overcome through decades of fierce persecution. We should
be helping them to face the new challenges of racism,
crime and unjust poverty.

A group of young Christian leaders gathered to
discuss how they should work in this post-communist
context. They asked me to sit with them, hear their
ideas (fortunately I speak some Russian) and add my
comments. It was a fascinating evening. When my turn
came, I noted they had said nothing about Christian
literature and suggested we should be producing good
books for evangelism, pastoral care, Bible teaching etc.
They listened politely, but said, 'You have not understood our situation. We don't want any literature.'

When I asked the reason, they added, 'Under communism anything printed was lying propaganda, so
Christian books will be understood in the same way.'

Another man then commented that actually anything said in front of other people was probably also
untrue. As a result they agreed that literature would be

useful, but somehow we have to write and to speak in such a way that we demonstrate our message is not untrue propaganda; the form must not be simplistic, the style openly sincere.

Our visits to Eastern Europe, Russia and ex-Soviet Central Asia have opened our eyes to new issues in the preaching, teaching and living the Christian faith.

China

Fifty years after Elizabeth's liberation from a Japanese prison camp in China, we visited the cities where she was born, went to school, was imprisoned and where her parents had worked as missionaries. Her father was a surgeon and superintendent of mission hospitals in Linfeng and Lanchow.

We were excited to meet leading Christians who had been converted and taught by Elizabeth's father and other missionaries of those days. I found it quite tear-jerking to see Elizabeth sitting on a bed next to an eighty-year-old lady who baby-sat for Elizabeth's parents when she was first born. And now she was the leader of a church with a thousand adults on a Sunday. I shall never forget their beaming faces as they looked into each other's eyes and held hands. Despite long years of horrendous persecution these old Christians stood firm for Christ and they have won through.

'The old China Inland Mission workers were the only people willing to live in a remote place like this', one Christian said to us. 'They set a pattern of suffering for Christ — and we have followed their example.'

It is true that the early missionaries did suffer much in order to spread the gospel through China. It is doubly true that since then Chinese believers have suffered infinitely more. We talked to several who had done 15–20 years hard labour in fearful camps. And many died for Christ under the Red Guards. But through it all the church has multiplied. Each church we went to was overflowing with crowds of people. But we noticed the great need for good expository Bible teaching. Church leaders are crying out for commentaries and teaching aids.

Regrettably we noticed that many expatriate workers in China do not have adequate knowledge of the Chinese language to be able to help Christians even with basic Bible teaching. As in so many countries, Christian workers require professional language teaching; at present we are rather amateur in language study.

The Muslim world

In the Muslim world everything depends on personal relationships. Legal rights and correct procedures pale into insignificance when compared with the importance of family connections or friendships. In our witness among Muslims therefore we have to concentrate on forming deep long-term friendships.

In a conference for workers in a North African country I talked with a woman who had served for over forty years in the same small town.

'As a midwife I brought nearly all of them into the world', she said with a smile. 'They have all crawled on my floor and eaten my biscuits as small children. They know and trust me. If they have problems at home or work, it is to me they come — I don't gossip and I'm their old friend.'

In North Africa and the Middle East several Christian workers have told me about people they have led to faith in Jesus Christ. Again and again the same sort of story emerges. Several years of friendship and Bible study together have led to a crunch decision; the cost of commitment to Christ has been too great and the Muslim has rejected both Jesus Christ and the Christian friend; after a further few years the Christian and the Muslim 'happen' to meet again and the process of friendship and Bible study begins again. This time it leads eventually to conversion. Altogether some ten years may have elapsed. If the Christian worker had only stayed short-term, the initial friendship would not have led finally to faith in Christ.

Long-term relationships are fundamental to the nature of God and the biblical revelation. The Father relates to the Son, the Son to the Spirit and God relates to humanity. In traditional theology we have studied the person and the work of Christ, but we ought also to look at the relationships of Christ — how does he relate to Jews, Samaritans and Gentiles? To men and women and children? To the rich and the poor? To people in power and to the weak, despised and oppressed? To his family, to the three close disciples, to the nine others and to the wider circle of his followers? To those who hate and oppose him?

In Muslim contexts we are compelled to rethink our traditional theological approaches. It seems to me that our theology will need to be expressed in more active and less abstract or systematic terms. Thus the fact that Jesus is the 'Word' in John 1 will not be looked at in terms of his divine-human nature, but in terms of words as God's means of creation and revealing communication. It is dynamic and active — God creates, reveals and communicates.

In Muslim countries I often hear how Christians are accused of being immoral because we allow women in our churches together with the men and we may have alcoholic drink.

'Christian men don't pray; they just look at the womens' legs', or, 'Christians drink wine or beer. Christians get drunk.' So run the accusations. Of course immoral sexual behaviour and drunkenness are common among western people who are only nominally Christian, and these sins can sometimes occur among bad Muslims too. But the accusations also assume that self-control is impossible. If men and women are together in a meeting, prayer is impossible and sexual lust is inevitable! If we drink one glass of wine, we shall lose control, drink more and become drunk! In reality the climactic fruit of the Holy Spirit in Galatians 5:23 is self-control. Because of the sanctifying work of the Holy Spirit both in Christians individually and corporately as the church, the accusations sound ridiculous in our ears. But they demonstrate the sad reality of a religion without the Holy Spirit.

In visits to Egypt and North Africa we have observed the position of the Berber and Nubian minorities, which are searching for their identity and significance. Surrounded by the Arab majorities they are often deemed second-class citizens. And yet they know that they were the original inhabitants of the area long before the Arab Muslim invasions.

In western Christian preaching we have often rejoiced in the reality that through Christ we can find our true worth individually. Is this not also true corporately? Should we not be advising community leaders among these peoples that Jesus Christ can give their people a new sense of identity?

This relates in a special way to the Nubians. They were a great Christian empire until just a few centuries ago, so their roots lie in the Christian faith. And when they were Christian, they held their heads high as a people. With Jesus Christ they could regain this dignity.

Despite the contemporary resurgence and growth of Islam around the world, we notice also a growing minority of Muslims who are disillusioned with the extremism and violence of fundamentalist Islamists. As a result a little trickle of Muslims are finding their way to faith in Christ — often through visions or dreams, miraculous healings or deliverance from curses and evil spirits, but also through personal witness and reading the Bible. As Christians we are called to witness, to distribute the scriptures and other Christian literature, and to pray that the Lord will reveal himself through dreams and miraculous demonstrations of his power.

The tragic consequences of extremist violence are seen most fearfully in Afghanistan. Different Muslim factions have been fighting each other ever since they defeated the Russians who had invaded their country.

I first visited Kabul back in 1980 when the Russians first entered the country, but the city is now almost unrecognizable. Most government buildings, the national museum, all the shopping areas and much of the residential housing have been totally destroyed by this Muslim in-fighting.

In the midst of the fighting one Christian worker found himself confronted by a local person who grabbed him by his shirt collars, shook him and shouted, 'Are you a Muslim?' Fearing that this was his end, the expatriate gave testimony that he believed in Jesus Christ.

'Promise me then that you will never become a Muslim,' shouted the man over the sound of rockets and bullets.

Some promises are easier than others to give!

During the worst of the fighting in Kabul all the world's media withdrew, as did also the United Nations personnel. But the Christian expatriate workers and the Red Cross remained. In the midst of the catastrophic destruction they have catered to the practical needs of the local population and the millions of refugees. Their credibility runs high. The testimony of their lives and work has joined hands with the witness of Christian radio to introduce Muslims to Jesus Christ. In this we must not forget the central role played by Afghan Christians whose faith is forged in the fire of fierce Muslim persecution.

My visits to Afghanistan with its unparalleled suffering have moved me deeply. It is a forgotten land and its sufferings only rarely get a mention in the media. I have felt called to pray and to call others to pray.

In much of the Muslim world Christian workers have to take seriously the threat of demonic attack. It may come in different forms, but I find that the most common is in a spirit of fear. National Christians and expatriates find that their witness is muted through this fear which goes beyond the caution which their circumstances require.

In my experience this contrasts markedly with Christians in the former communist world, who shared their faith boldly in the midst of ferocious persecution. For example, I met a group of four men who went from village to village singing about Christ. They knew that this was illegal according to the communist law. Finally they were duly arrested and put in prison. One of them told me how his nine-year-old son visited him in prison and announced, 'Don't worry, Daddy, a group of my friends and I are carrying on your work. We are going from one village to another and telling them about Jesus.'

It's no wonder that the church in those countries has overcome all adversities and won the day. Similarly, in the Muslim world Christians need a combination of love, wisdom and boldness.

Europe

As a Jew from a family which originated in Germany, visits to that country gain special significance. The key words of the Christian gospel take on new meaning — 'forgiveness', 'reconciliation', 'atonement', 'peace', 'love' etc.

'The blood of Jesus cleanses us from *all* sin.' My arms embraced the heaving shoulders of a well-dressed German Christian as he sobbed his confession. In one of the worst concentration camps he had whipped long lines of naked Jews into gas chambers. His past haunted him in constant nightmares. As a good Christian he knew well the verse I quoted, but still he could never feel its reality. Was his past sin beyond the possibility of forgiveness? Cleansing and relief came to him as he heard from Jewish lips the assured promise that the blood of Jesus cleanses us not just of some sin, but from *all* sin.

The aftermath of the Nazi Holocaust can still bring spiritual hardening and darkness in Germany. Young people wonder what their parents were doing at that time and relationships suffer.

'Don't blame me! I didn't do anything!' an evangelical church elder ranted at me in a loud voice for some ten minutes while his daughter listened with horror. Nobody had said anything about the Nazi era, but guilt oozed from him and his protestations without confession made his family despise him.

Gradually the fires of the gas chambers dim and become mere history. A new openness can penetrate German society. One wonders whether now the good news of Jesus Christ may move forwards and the churches regain spiritual vitality.

But Germany faces formidable hurdles against the gospel. The weight of liberal criticism and of non-Christian philosophy hangs heavy over the theological faculties, the churches and indeed the nation's thinking. Karl Marx pointed out that the German people have a tendency to separate thinking and doing — those who do anything don't think, while those who think don't do anything! Of course such a generalization is over-simple and not entirely true, but such tendencies can hinder the life of the church.

I always find my visits to Germany a challenge, but also a great privilege. My German friends and associates hold a special place in my heart. God does bring reconciliation and makes his people one in Christ!

In the midst of a travelling ministry we have found it helpful to have certain fixed points. Our relationships at All Nations, in our local church and community give a firm base from which we can go out. Then too we go each year to three countries — Korea, Norway and Sweden. Again we feel this gives us a certain rooted stability in what could otherwise become a restless existence.

We started lecturing each year at the Orebro Theological Seminary back in 1980. On my first visit I was graciously invited to an evening meal together with all the faculty at the principal's house. Everyone was on their best behaviour as we sipped cool drinks in the lounge before dinner was served. Eventually it was announced that the meal was ready and I was ushered into the dining room first. The polished table gleamed, the cutlery and glass sparkled as they lay alongside the fine china, silver candlesticks stood proudly next to two large prawn dishes — and the cat lurked guiltily on the table, having scattered the prawn shapes all over the place!

All formality came to an end. More intimate personal friendships began and I have felt at home there ever since. Cats have their uses!

Orebro is a beautiful city and we look forward to our annual visits. The thick-walled twelfth century castle dominates the town centre with the river flowing around it. Every year I love to walk along the river, enjoying the old Swedish buildings along its banks and then looking up at the impressive towers of the castle.

In a different way the Santal Mission Bible school in Norway also has great beauty. Carved out of the forest next to a typical Norwegian lake its traditional red-painted houses nestle below the wooded hills.

In previous generations Norwegian theologians under the leadership of Professor Hallesby resisted the inroads of destructive liberalism with the result that the Lutheran state Church remained evangelical. Unlike the rest of Europe secularism and liberalism have only recently undermined the spiritual life of the church. With the accompanying spiritual uncertainty and loss of vital faith people have felt the need for forming new churches which can be definitely evangelical. This has led to the emergence of more free churches, which were not felt necessary before. But the majority of the people still hold firmly to the Lutheran Church.

It was in Norway that I faced in a new way the issue of a Christian attitude to violence. My wife's mother was Norwegian and she still has many relatives there. On our first visit to Norway we met an old uncle and his wife. They were very artistic, living in a little house filled with their paintings and sculptures. They spent their time playing violin and piano in concert together. One day we asked them about their life in the second World War.

'I put explosives on the railway tracks and blew up German troop-trains', explained Uncle Asbjorn. We could hardly imagine this sensitive Christian involved in such activities. I had to ask myself when does violence become a Christian virtue and when is it a sin? As a Jew, would I have used a gun against Hitler?

Throughout Northern Europe we battle with the pressing issue of the Christian understanding of other faiths. While Jewish evangelization has become the focal point of the debate, it relates to evangelistic mission among people of any non-Christian faith. With the growth of ethnic minority communities in all our European countries this has become the burning issue. Do we still really believe that God has revealed himself uniquely in Jesus Christ, God become flesh and living amongst us? Do we believe that the death, resurrection and ascension of Jesus Christ form God's particular way of salvation? If so, then how can we deny anybody the opportunity to enjoy salvation and the fulness of life in Christ?

But does such an emphasis on our evangelistic calling lead us into an unacceptable arrogance and intolerance? Can we remain confident of truth in Christ and yet remain humble and loving? Can we also still be open to learn from the goodness and truth to be found within other faiths and their followers?

It seems to me that the church will stand or fall by our answers to these questions.

Southern Europe

One advantage of getting older is that church history becomes one's own personal experience!

When I was a student (which war was that before?!) many of us were called of God to pray fervently for mission opportunities in Latin America. Various of my friends went as missionaries to that continent. In those days there were very few Protestant Christians there and the Roman Catholic Church languished in a pre-Reformation-style mixture of Christianity and traditional tribal religion. Persecution of Protestants burned fiercely.

When the Holy Spirit stirred people to pray and to go as missionaries, he had a definite purpose. God wanted to work abundantly in that continent — and now we think of Latin America as a continent of dynamic fast-growing churches.

Then God moved on. He gave the church worldwide a passionate concern for the communist world. Brother Andrew's *God's Smuggler* became a best-seller. The Holy Spirit led his people to pray for persecuted Christians and for evangelistic ministries beyond the iron curtain. Now the curtain has been torn down, relative freedom has returned to those lands and the church has flourished. When God calls to prayer and sends people in mission, he clearly has definite purposes in mind.

In more recent years in every continent God has given the church a deep concern for the Muslim world. Much prayer rises to God for Muslims and increasing numbers of Christian workers dedicate their lives to mission in Muslim countries. We begin to see God at work. A small trickle of Muslims are coming into life-changing faith in Christ. But there still remains much to be done if we are to see that trickle becoming a mighty flood. Nevertheless it has started.

So we ask ourselves what will be God's next move. When the Muslim world opens the floodgates to the gospel, which part of the world will God call us all to pray for and to go to in mission?

I wonder if it will be Southern Europe.

The small evangelical churches of those countries are tempted to live as irrelevant ghettos in the midst of a sea of traditional Roman Catholicism or Greek Orthodoxy. Defensive legalism can divide them from the people they ought to be evangelizing. Sectarian emphasis on their denominational affiliation or their charismatic/non-charismatic stance can also separate them from each other. Relatively minor issues may replace Jesus Christ as the centre of their faith and spiritual life.

But these churches are the body and the bride of Christ. There can be no doubt that Jesus loves his bride! It may therefore be dangerous for us to be too critical or to by-pass these national churches. They are his chosen people, precious to him. They are his special instrument for the spread of his good news.

Although the countries of Southern Europe are called 'Roman Catholic' or 'Orthodox', in practice they are increasingly secular and materialistic with flourishing pagan and spiritist movements. At the same time we rejoice to see renewal movements struggling for growth in the traditional Catholic and Orthodox Churches. A small minority is regaining a love for Jesus Christ at the centre of their faith with new emphasis on Bible reading.

Southern Europe awaits God's call to his church in every continent to pray and to go in mission. Then we shall look forward to a new movement of the Holy Spirit in that part of the world too.

Conclusion

So we come back to where we started — what sort of legacy do we want to pass on to others? How can we summarize the many lessons which God has wanted to teach us?

We look back on all the vicissitudes of life with the testimony that in Christ 'all things hold together' (Col. 1:17) — wonderfully everything fits into place and makes sense. Those words of Paul lead on to the emphasis which we desire to be at the heart of our lives and central to the legacy we pass on — 'that in everything he might be pre-eminent'.

We have come to realize how easily we put ourselves or other things in the first place in our lives. I have preached frequently on this subject, warning Christians not to put their denominational or personal emphases into the place of Christ as the pinnacle of Christian faith.

It is sometimes said that, if a preacher constantly underlines one particular sin in their sermons, you may be sure that is a particular temptation to them! So it was with me! God's Holy Spirit showed me that I was guilty of the very sin I warned against.

My life has been dedicated to the spread of the gospel of Christ through Christian mission. I came to see that mission had become central in my life rather than Christ himself. Of course Jesus was useful in encouraging people to commit their energies to mission! I needed to reverse this. Mission should be glorifying Christ, not Christ as a servant to promote mission.

The legacy I want to pass on to others is indeed that all of us should live for the glory of Jesus Christ alone. In this context I long to encourage people to engage whole-heartedly in mission to spread his kingdom. I pray that the lessons God has wanted to teach me may also encourage and stimulate many others to live more fully for the glory of Christ all over the world.